india &
pakistan

To Reuben, who married me before I learned to cook.

Completely revised and updated in 2011
First published in 1976

This edition published in 2013 by Hardie Grant Books

Hardie Grant Books (Australia)
Ground Floor, Building 1
658 Church Street
Richmond, Victoria 3121
www.hardiegrant.com.au

Hardie Grant Books (UK)
Dudley House, North Suite
34–35 Southampton Street
London WC2E 7HF
www.hardiegrant.co.uk

A Cataloguing-in-Publication entry is available from the catalogue of the National Library of
Australia at www.nla.gov.au
The Complete Asian Cookbook: India and Pakistan
ISBN 978 1 74270 686 3

Publishing Director: Paul McNally
Project Editor: Helen Withycombe
Editor: Ariana Klepac
Design Manager: Heather Menzies
Design Concept: Murray Batten
Typesetting: Megan Ellis
Photographer: Alan Benson
Stylist: Vanessa Austin
Production: Todd Rechner

Colour reproduction by Splitting Image Colour Studio
Printed and bound in China by 1010 Printing International Limited

Find this book on **Cooked.**

THE
Complete
Asian
COOKBOOK

india &

pakistan

CHARMAINE SOLOMON

hardie grant books
MELBOURNE · LONDON

Contents

Foreword

Just as France has its robust country fare as well as its subtle haute cuisine, so too does Asia have a range of culinary delights that can be simple, complex, fiery, mild, tantalising — and compulsive! Not all Asian food is exotic or wildly unusual. Noodle and rice dishes are as commonplace as the pastas and potatoes of the West. Many of the ingredients will be familiar to anyone who knows their way around a kitchen. The main differences have arisen just as they have arisen in other parts of the world — through the use of available ingredients. Thus there is a reliance on some herbs and spices less well known in the West. Meat is often replaced by the nutritious by-products of the soy bean and by protein-rich fish sauces and shrimp pastes.

True, some of the more unusual ingredients take a little getting used to. But once you have overcome what resistance you may have towards the idea of raw fish or dried shrimp paste or seaweed, you'll find that these (and other) ingredients are no less delicious than – and certainly as exciting as – those you use in your favourite dishes.

The introduction to this book will give you a good idea of what to expect in the way of out-of-the-ordinary ingredients. Almost without exception, those called for are readily available in most large supermarkets or Asian grocery stores; in the rare case they are not, suitable substitutes have been given.

Those of you already familiar with Indian and Pakistani cuisines will, I hope, find recipes to interest and excite you in these pages; and I think you will be tempted to explore cuisines with which you are less well acquainted. For those of you who are coming to South Asian cooking for the first time, I have taken care to make sure the essential steps are clear and precise, with detailed instructions on the following pages for cooking the much-used ingredients (such as rice, coconut milk and chilli), and pointers on how to joint a chicken and portion fish.

For most recipes, the names have been given in Hindi, followed by the English name in italics. Don't be surprised to see the word 'mutton' – it was adopted by the Indians from the British in the same way that the latter adopted *topee* and *pukka* and many other Indian words.

Eating for health

Most Asian food is healthy. Many spices and ingredients such as turmeric, garlic and ginger have proven health-giving properties. However, with today's emphasis on weight control I have made modifications in the quantity and type of fat used for cooking. I have found it is possible to get very good results using almost half the amount of fat called for in many traditional dishes.

Ghee, or clarified butter, is the main cooking medium in North India. It keeps without refrigeration because it is pure butterfat with all the milk solids removed. It is essential both for flavour and for its ability to reach high temperatures without burning. I use it for flavour, but substitute light oils for a proportion of the ghee. In some recipes it is not possible to use substitutes without spoiling the end product – for instance, in Indian sweetmeats or biscuits (cookies) such as *nan khatai*. Don't substitute margarine or vegetable shortening in these recipes, for you will not get the desired results.

All of these recipes are adaptable to low-fat diets with very little sacrifice of flavour, since most of the exotic tastes come from herbs, spices and sauces.

Deep-frying

To check the temperature for deep-frying, use a kitchen thermometer if you have one – on average, 180°C (350°F) is the correct temperature. To test without a thermometer, a cube of bread dropped into the oil will brown in 15 seconds at 180°C (350°F), and in 10 seconds if the temperature is 190°C (375°F).

The higher temperature may be suitable to use for foods that don't have great thickness, such as pappadams, but if something needs to cook through, such as chicken pieces, use a lower temperature of around 160°C (320°F) – in this case a cube of bread will take nearly 30 seconds to brown. If the temperature is not hot enough, the food will absorb oil and become greasy. If you overheat the oil it could catch fire.

Use refined peanut oil, light olive oil, canola or rice bran oil and lower the food in gently with tongs or a slotted spoon so as not to splash yourself with hot oil. Removing the fried food to a colander lined with crumpled paper towel will help to remove any excess oil.

After cooling, oil may be poured through a fine metal skimmer and stored in an airtight jar away from the light. It may be used within a month or so, adding fresh oil to it when heating. After a couple of uses, it will need to be disposed of properly.

Coconut milk

I have heard many people refer to the clear liquid inside a coconut as 'coconut milk'. I have even read it in books. So, at the risk of boring those who already know, let's establish right away what coconut milk really is. It's the milky liquid extracted from the grated flesh of mature fresh coconuts or reconstituted from desiccated (shredded) coconut.

Coconut milk is an important ingredient in the cookery of nearly all Asian countries. It is used in soups, curries, savoury meat or seafood mixtures and all kinds of desserts. It has an unmistakable flavour and richness and should be used in recipes that call for it.

When the first edition of this book was published in 1975, the only good way to obtain coconut milk outside the countries where coconuts grow was to extract it yourself. These days coconut milk is widely available in tins from supermarkets. Problematically, the quality between brands varies enormously so it is worth comparing a few brands and checking the ingredients list – it should only have coconut and water in it. It should smell and taste fresh and clean and be neither watery nor solid. It is better to avoid brands that include stabilisers and preservatives. Shake the tin well before opening to disperse the richness evenly throughout. Brands in Tetra Paks tend not to be lumpy or watery.

Delicious as it is, coconut milk is full of saturated fat. With this in mind, I suggest that only when coconut cream is required should you use the tinned coconut milk undiluted. Where a recipe calls for thick coconut milk, dilute the tinned product with half its volume in water (for example, 250 ml/8½ fl oz/1 cup tinned coconut milk and 125 ml/4 fl oz/½ cup water). Where coconut milk is required, dilute the tinned coconut milk with an equal amount of water. Where thin coconut milk is required, dilute the tinned coconut milk with two parts by volume of water (for example, 250 ml/8½ fl oz/1 cup tinned coconut milk and 500 ml/17 fl oz/2 cups water).

If you would like to make your own coconut milk, the extraction method is included below. Traditionally, coconut milk is extracted in two stages – the first yield being the 'thick milk', the second extraction producing 'thin milk'. Use a mixture of first and second extracts when a recipe calls for coconut milk unless thick milk or thin milk is specified. Sometimes they are added at different stages of the recipe. Some recipes use 'coconut cream'. This is the rich layer that rises to the top of the thick milk (or first extract) after it has been left to stand for a while.

Making coconut milk from scratch

Using desiccated (shredded) coconut

Makes 375 ml (12½ fl oz/1½ cups) thick coconut milk
Makes 500 ml (17 fl oz/2 cups) thin coconut milk

Many cooks use desiccated coconut for making coconut milk. It is much easier and quicker to prepare than grating fresh coconut, and in curries you cannot tell the difference.

180 g (6½ oz/2 cups) desiccated (shredded) coconut

1.25 litres (42 fl oz/5 cups) hot water

Put the desiccated coconut into a large bowl and pour over 625 ml (21 fl oz/2½ cups) of the hot water then allow to cool to lukewarm. Knead firmly with your hands for a few minutes, then strain through a fine sieve or a piece of muslin (cheesecloth), pressing or squeezing out as much liquid as possible; this is the thick coconut milk.

Repeat the process using the same coconut and remaining hot water. This extract will yield the thin coconut milk. (Because of the moisture retained in the coconut the first time, the second extract usually yields more milk.)

Alternatively, to save time, you can use an electric blender or food processor. Put the desiccated coconut and 625 ml (21 fl oz/2½ cups) of the hot water into the blender and process for 30 seconds, then strain through a fine sieve or piece of muslin (cheesecloth), squeezing out all the moisture. Repeat, using the same coconut and remaining hot water.

Note: *Sometimes a richer milk is required. For this, hot milk replaces the water and only the first extract is used. However, a second extract will yield a flavoursome and reasonably rich grade of coconut milk that can be used in soups, curries or other dishes.*

Using fresh coconut

Makes 375 ml (12½ fl oz/1½ cups) thick coconut milk
Makes 500 ml (17 fl oz/2 cups) thin coconut milk

In Asian countries, fresh coconut is used and a coconut grater is standard equipment in every household. Grating fresh coconut is easy if you have the right implement for the job. However, if you are able to get fresh coconuts and do not have such an implement, use a food processor to pulverise the coconut and then extract the milk.

1 fresh coconut

1 litre (34 fl oz/4 cups) water or milk

Preheat the oven to 180°C (350°F). Crack the coconut in half by hitting it with the back of a heavy kitchen chopper. Once a crack has appeared, insert the thin edge of the blade and prise it open. Save the sweet liquid inside for drinking. If you do not own a coconut grater, put the two halves on a baking tray and bake in the oven for 15–20 minutes, or until the flesh starts to come away from the shell. Lift it out with the point of a knife, and peel away the thin dark brown skin that clings to the white portion. Cut into chunks.

Put the coconut flesh into a food processor with 500 ml (17 fl oz/2 cups) of the water and process until the coconut is completely pulverised. Strain the liquid using a sieve or muslin (cheesecloth) to extract the thick coconut milk. Repeat this process using the same coconut and remaining water to extract the thin milk. Left-over freshly extracted or bought coconut milk may be frozen – ice cube trays are ideal.

Chillies

Fresh chillies are used in most Asian food. If mild flavouring is required, simply wash the chilli and add it to the dish when simmering, then lift out and discard the chilli before serving. But if you want the authentic fiery quality of the dish, you need to seed and chop the chillies first. To do this, remove the stalk of each chilli and cut in half lengthways to remove the central membrane and seeds – the seeds are the hottest part of the chilli. If you wish to make fiery hot sambals, the chillies are used seeds and all – generally ground or puréed in a food processor.

If you handle chillies without wearing gloves, wash your hands thoroughly with soap and warm water afterwards. Chillies can be so hot that even two or three good washings do not stop the tingling sensation, which can go on for hours. If this happens, remember to keep your hands well away from your eyes, lips or where the skin is especially sensitive. If you have more chillies than you need, they can be wrapped in plastic wrap and frozen, then added to dishes and used without thawing.

Dried chillies come in many shapes and sizes. Generally I use the large variety. If frying them as an accompaniment to a meal, use them whole, dropping them straight into hot oil. If they are being soaked and ground as part of the spicing for a sambal, sauce or curry, first cut off the stalk end and shake the chilli so that the seeds fall out. They are safe enough to handle until they have been soaked and ground, but if you handle them after this has been done, remember to wash your hands at once with soap and water.

Dried chillies, though they give plenty of heat and flavour, do not have the same volatile oils as fresh chillies and so do not have as much effect on the skin.

Rice varieties

One of the oldest grains in the world, and a staple food of more than half the world's population, rice is by far the most important item in the daily diet throughout Asia.

There are thousands of varieties. Agricultural scientists involved in producing new and higher yielding strains of rice will pick differences that are not apparent to even the most enthusiastic rice eater. But, from the Asian consumer's viewpoint, rice has qualities that a Westerner might not even notice – colour, fragrance, flavour, texture.

Rice buyers are so trained to recognise different types of rice that they can hold a few grains in the palm to warm it, sniff it through the hole made by thumb and forefinger, and know its age, variety, even perhaps where it was grown. Old rice is sought after and prized more than new rice because it tends to be fluffy and separate when cooked, even if the cook absent-mindedly adds too much water. Generally speaking, the white polished grains – whether long and fine or small and pearly (much smaller than what we know as short-grain rice) – are considered best.

The desirable features of rice are not the same in every Asian country. In India and Pakistan, fluffy, dry rice is preferred. Long, thin grains are considered best and rice is cooked with salt. The most dreadful thing a cook could do is forget to salt the rice.

Rice is sold either packaged or in bulk. Polished white rice is available as long-, medium- or short-grain. Unpolished or natural rice is available as medium- or long-grain; and in many countries it is possible to buy an aromatic table rice grown in Bangladesh, called basmati rice. In dishes where spices and flavourings are added and cooked with the rice, any type of long-grain rice may be used. In each recipe the type of rice best suited is recommended, but as a general rule, remember that medium-grain or short-grain rice gives a clinging result and long-grain rice, properly cooked, is fluffy and separate.

Preparing rice

To wash or not to wash? Among Asian cooks there will never be agreement on whether rice should be washed or not. Some favour washing the rice several times, then leaving it to soak for a while. Other good cooks insist that washing rice is stupid and wasteful, taking away what vitamins and nutrients are left after the milling process.

I have found that most rice sold in Australia does not need washing but that rice imported in bulk and packaged here picks up a lot of dust and dirt and needs thorough washing and draining.

In a recipe, if rice is to be fried before any liquid is added, the washed rice must be allowed enough time to thoroughly drain and dry, between 30 and 60 minutes. Rice to be steamed must be soaked overnight. Rice for cooking by the absorption method may be washed (or not), drained briefly and added to the pan immediately.

Cooking rice

For a fail-safe way of cooking rice perfectly every time, put the required amount of rice and water into a large saucepan with a tight-fitting lid (see the measures on page 10). Bring to the boil over high heat, cover, then reduce the heat to low and simmer for 20 minutes. Remove from the heat, uncover the pan and allow the steam to escape for a few minutes before fluffing up the rice with a fork.

Transfer the rice to a serving dish with a slotted metal spoon – don't use a wooden spoon or it will crush the grains. You will notice that long-grain rice absorbs considerably more water than short-grain rice, so the two kinds are not interchangeable in recipes. Though details are given in every rice recipe, here is a general rule regarding proportions of rice and liquid.

Long-grain rice

200 g (7 oz/1 cup) rice use 500 ml
  (17 fl oz/2 cups) water

400 g (14 oz/2 cups) rice use 875 ml
  (29½ fl oz/3½ cups) water

600 g (1 lb 5 oz/3 cups) rice use
  1.25 litres (42 fl oz/5 cups) water

Use 500 ml (17 fl oz/2 cups) water for the first cup of rice, then 375 ml
  (12½ fl oz/1½ cups) water for each additional cup of rice.

Short- or medium-grain rice

220 g (8 oz/1 cup) rice use 375 ml
  (12½ fl oz/1½ cups) water

440 g (15½ oz/2 cups) rice use 625 ml
  (21 fl oz/2½ cups) water

660 g (1 lb 7 oz/3 cups) rice use 875 ml
  (29½ fl oz/3½ cups) water

Use 375 ml (12½ fl oz/1½ cups) water
  for the first cup of rice, then 250 ml
  (8½ fl oz/1 cup) water for each additional cup of rice.

Preparing whole chickens

Jointing a chicken

I have often referred to cutting a chicken into serving pieces suitable for a curry. This is simply cutting the pieces smaller than joints so that the spices can more readily penetrate and flavour the meat.

To joint a chicken, first cut off the thighs and drumsticks, then separate the drumsticks from the thighs. Cut off the wings and divide them at the middle joint (wing tips may be added to a stock but do not count as a joint). The breast is divided down the centre into two, then across into four pieces – do not start cooking the breast pieces at the same time as the others, but add them later, as breast meat has a tendency to become dry if cooked for too long.

A 1.5 kg (3 lb 5 oz) chicken, for instance, can be jointed, then broken down further into serving pieces. The thighs are cut into two with a heavy cleaver; the back is cut into four pieces and used in the curry, though not counted as serving pieces because there is very little meat on them. Neck and giblets are also included to give extra flavour.

Preparing whole fish

Cutting fish fillets into serving pieces

Fish fillets are of varying thickness, length and density. For example, whole fillets of flathead can be dipped in tempura batter and will cook in less than a minute in hot oil, whereas a fillet of ling or trevalla will need to be cut into 3 cm (1¼ in) strips for the same recipe.

Let common sense prevail when portioning fish fillets, but always remember that fish is cooked when the flesh turns opaque when flaked with a fork or knife.

Cutting fish steaks into serving pieces

Depending on the size of the fish, each steak may need to be cut into four, six or eight pieces. Once again, smaller portions are better, for they allow flavours to penetrate and you can allow more than one piece per person. The accompanying sketch shows how to divide fish steaks – small ones into four pieces, medium-sized ones into six pieces and really large steaks into eight pieces.

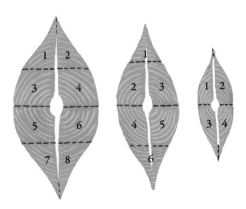

India & Pakistan

Most Westerners, when asked what food they associate with the Indian subcontinent, will say 'curry', but not every spiced dish is a curry, and curry is not just one dish. It embraces a whole range of dishes, each distinctly different according to the spices and herbs used in varying combinations.

Spices, imaginatively used, are the outstanding feature of Indian and Pakistani cookery – subtle or pungent, hot or mild, there is something to suit every palate.

Much of the cooking of northwestern India and Pakistan (formerly West Pakistan) is so similar that I, for one, would hesitate to say which dishes belong to one country and which to the other. Pakistan, being a Muslim country, uses no pork but it boasts a diet rich in other meats and has as many sumptuous birianis and pilaus as does the celebrated Moghul cuisine of the neighbouring Indian provinces. Lamb is predominant in both countries, and both use spicing and ingredients such as yoghurt and ghee in dishes that are elaborate without being hot; both, too, rely more heavily on wheat-flour chapatis than on rice.

Bangladesh (formerly East Pakistan) is more than 1500 kilometres (900 miles) from Pakistan. With the eastern Indian province of Bengal, of which it was once a part, it shares more pungent spicing, a tendency to cook in mustard oil rather than ghee, and places an emphasis on a variety of seafood instead of lamb.

The culinary offerings of southern India are different again. The coconut plays a commanding role, rice largely replaces wheat, mustard seeds are widely used as a spice, and chillies come into their own – as anyone who has tackled a really hot Madras or Mysore curry will readily acknowledge!

Throughout the subcontinent, different religions impose food taboos that are rigidly adhered to: Hindus will not eat beef, Muslims will not eat pork, Buddhists will not take life and some will not even crack an egg. Many Indians are strictly vegetarian, enjoying a cuisine that is in a class by itself and which could convert the most dedicated meat eater. It includes superb curries; *bartha* (purées) and *bhaji* (fried vegetables); *pakorha* (fritters) and *vadai* (rissoles of lentils and pulses); homemade bread with spiced vegetable fillings; high-protein dishes based on lentils and homemade cheeses; and rich sweetmeats made with vegetables and fruit.

When I think of Indian sweets I think of an Indian sweetmaker I knew. He was over six feet (180 centimetres) tall, had a ruddy complexion, dark hair and dark flashing eyes. I guessed his age at around sixty, but he stood erect and looked strong and healthy; he was one of the proudest, most dignified men I have ever met. I cannot remember ever seeing him smile. While not surly, he saw no reason to smile at his customers. Was it not enough that they were able to purchase the exquisite work of his hands?

His shop, which was nestled close to a Hindu temple covered by stone carvings of gods, goddesses, mortals and animals, was stark and unrelieved by any kind of decoration. Inside, there was only a glass showcase to protect the sweetmeats from the ever-present flies. Further inside, partly hidden by a curtain, was the small stone fireplace on the stone floor where he squatted on his heels to prepare his delicacies. In the bazaar area were a variety of lesser sweets, but he made only the expensive, exquisite, rich varieties and his clientele knew they were privileged to taste the work of a master craftsman and cheerfully paid his high prices.

Eastern sweetmakers are a race unto themselves. They guard their secrets as jealously as they guard their money and yet, somehow, the secrets leak out. Recipes, good and not quite so good, are printed in cookbooks. But they are no great threat to the sweetmakers, for who would take the trouble to make these morsels? As long as I lived in the East, I was content to buy the sweetmeats. But when we settled in a Western country at a time when such sweets were unobtainable, I knew it was necessary to do something about it.

And so began the search for recipes, the repeated experiments, the ultimate triumph. Was it worth it? Oh yes! Once you have tasted rose and cardamom-scented *rasgula*, *barfi* and *gulab jaman*, you will not rest until you know that you can make the glorious confections yourself. If you have a sweet tooth and a taste for the exotic, you will enjoy these recipes as much as I do.

Serving and eating Indian and Pakistani meals

In southern India, banana leaves are often used as plates, but more universal is the *thali* service – the thali being a circular metal tray on which are placed a number of small bowls called *katori*, also made of metal. Rice or chapatis are placed directly on the tray; curries and other accompaniments are served in the bowls. The food is eaten with the fingers of the right hand only, for it is considered impolite to use the 'unclean' left hand to touch food.

Some orthodox Hindus feel that spoons, forks and plates that are used again and again are quite unhygienic, but in most Indian cities Western customs have taken over and food is served on dinner plates and eaten with a spoon and fork.

Rice is served first in the centre of the plate, then various curries and accompaniments are placed around it. The rice is the base, and only one curry should be tasted with each mouthful of rice in order to appreciate the individual spicing of each dish.

The matter of proportions is all-important. One needs to forget the Western idea of a large amount of meat or fish with a small amount of rice. Rice is the main part of the meal and curries of meat, fish or vegetables should be served in much smaller portions. There is wisdom in this too, because when food is spiced it needs the bland background of rice to delight the palate and placate the digestion.

When eating Indian breads with a meal, there is no choice but to eat with one's fingers. Tear off a piece of chapati or paratha, use it to scoop up the accompaniment, fold it over neatly, then eat it. Just as Chinese or Japanese food tastes better eaten with chopsticks, Indian food tastes better eaten with the fingers. Finger bowls are provided, of course.

One of the other main features that sets an Indian meal apart is the number and variety of accompaniments to the main dishes. In fact, these accompaniments are as important as the main meal itself. They include dried fish or pappadams (lentil wafers), fresh chutneys made from herbs, coconut, acid fruits and other ingredients; and also bland cooling yoghurt raitas. These raitas are called *pachchadis* in South India, and incorporate more spicy seasoning.

An Indian salad presupposes hot chillies as an ingredient, or a sufficient sprinkling of chilli powder to give it a 'kick'. If the raw vegetables are dressed with enough chilli, then the salad becomes a sambal. Use your imagination and create raitas, salads and chutneys from fruit and vegetables in season. For cooked chutneys see pages 166–70; these chutneys, though popular with Westerners, are almost unknown in India.

Other popular accompaniments include Bombay duck (glossary), dried sprats, fried nuts, grated coconut or fresh fruits. Ripe bananas are served, sliced and sprinkled with lemon juice, as a foil to a very hot curry. They may be served raw or cut into chunks and fried, and take the place of a sweet chutney.

Unripe mangoes, stones removed, peeled and sliced, sprinkled with salt and chilli powder, are also served as an accompaniment, like a fresh chutney. Ripe mangoes are never served with a curry meal, but may follow as a dessert. Half-ripe pineapple is another favourite fruit accompaniment. The 'eyes' are removed, the flesh is diced and then sprinkled with salt and chilli powder.

What to drink with an Indian meal has always been the subject of much argument. Cold water is the most authentic, but many Indians prefer a sweet drink such as *sharbat gulab* or *falooda*. Even *lassi*, the cooling yoghurt drink, may be offered in sweet and salty versions. It can be simply sweetened, flavoured with mango or spiced with cardamom and rosewater or served salty using garam masala. These are certainly effective in quenching fiery spices. For those who want an alcoholic beverage, a chilled lager or shandy, or wine cup filled with a semi-sweet white wine or rosé is permissible, but fine dry wines and curries just do not go together. One warning: carbonated or 'fizzy' drinks, including lager beer, tend to exaggerate the burning sensation of a really hot curry, as does ice-cold water.

Utensils

The well-equipped modern kitchen with gas or electric stoves, blenders, coffee grinders, refrigerators and freezers makes cooking much easier than it is in a traditional Indian kitchen.

The brass *degchi* used throughout India is like a saucepan without handles. The sides are straight and have a horizontal rim. The flat lid fits over the rim of the pan, and is sometimes sealed with a flour and water paste, making a sort of oven or steam cooker out of the pan, for what is called *dum* cooking. Hot coals are put on the lid to provide cooking heat from above as well as below, for ovens are almost unknown in the average Indian household. Nowadays the degchi is also made from aluminium.

Saucepans with well-fitting lids are just as suitable as a degchi, and a casserole in the oven is the answer to dum cooking. Wooden spoons substitute for the coconut-shell spoons mostly used in India, and a deep frying pan takes the place of the *karahi*, a rounded pan used for frying. A griddle or heavy iron plate replaces the *tawa* on which chapatis or paratha are cooked; even a heavy frying pan will do. The ever-present grinding stone for spices, and the coconut grater, are replaced by the versatile electric blender, a coffee mill used to grind spices only or failing that, a mortar and pestle.

Common ingredients

Garam masala

Meaning, literally, 'hot spice', this is a staple blend for your Indian spice shelf. There are many versions of garam masala, some using hot spices, such as pepper, and others only the fragrant spices. If stored in an airtight container away from heat and light, garam masala will stay flavoursome and fragrant for 6 months or longer and amply repay the effort of making it. Here again, if you find a good commercial garam masala, by all means use it – but if you are a real enthusiast about spice cookery, you owe it to yourself to try a homemade blend or two. They are so marvellously adaptable to your own taste.

Ghee

Clarified butter or pure butterfat, ghee is what gives the rich, distinctive flavour to north Indian cooking. Having no milk solids, it can be heated to much higher temperatures than butter without burning. It is sold in tins, packets or tubs. If you find it difficult to buy ghee, make your own by heating butter in a saucepan until it melts and froths. Spoon the foam off the top and pour the melted butter into a heatproof glass bowl, discarding the milk solids in the pan. Leave to cool to room temperature, then chill until set. Spoon off the fat from the top. Heat the fat again, then strain through fine muslin (cheesecloth) to remove any remaining solids. This ghee will keep for 3 to 4 months without refrigeration.

Khoa

Used to make Indian sweetmeats, khoa is unsweetened condensed milk made by boiling milk quickly in a shallow pan (such as a large, heavy-based frying pan) to allow for as much surface evaporation as possible. It must be stirred constantly. When ready, khoa has the consistency of uncooked pastry. One litre (34 fl oz/4 cups) milk yields about 90 g (3 oz) khoa.

Malai

Malai is thick cream. This is not the separated cream sold commercially, but it is collected from the top of the milk. The milk is kept boiling steadily in a wide pan, usually with a fan playing on the surface to cool the top of the milk and hasten formation of the skin. When cool, the skin is removed and the process repeated. It is possible to buy this type of cream from Middle Eastern grocery stores, where it is called *ashtar*.

Cooking oils

Different oils used in various parts of India give the cookery of each region a distinctive flavour. *Til*, or sesame oil, and coconut oil are much used in southern India, while in Bengal the favourite cooking medium is mustard oil. It is up to your personal taste what type of oil you use, but extra-virgin olive oil is not used in Indian cooking. Maize, sunflower or light olive oil are the best substitutes and may be flavoured with ghee.

Panch phora

'Panch' means five in Hindi, and *panch phora* is a combination of five different aromatic seeds. These are used whole and, when added to the cooking oil, impart a flavour typical of certain Indian dishes. Combine 2 tablespoons each of black mustard seed, cumin seed and nigella seed and 1 tablespoon each of fenugreek seed and fennel seed. Store in an airtight jar and shake before using. There is no substitute.

Panir

Panir is homemade cream cheese. To make your own, bring milk to the boil, stirring occasionally to prevent a skin forming on top. As the milk starts to rise in the pan, stir in lemon juice in the proportion of 1 tablespoon to 625 ml (21 fl oz/2½ cups) milk. Remove from the heat and let stand for 5 minutes, by which time firm curds will have formed. Strain through muslin (cheesecloth) and leave to hang for at least 30 minutes, then press to remove as much moisture as possible. If it has to be very firm, weight it down and leave for some hours in a cool place (this is necessary when it is to be cut into cubes and cooked with vegetable dishes, such as in Mattar panir on page 142). It may be added to any of the vegetable preparations for extra nutrition.

Rice

The preferred rice in Indian, especially Moghul, cooking is basmati rice. Its long, fragrant grains make perfectly fluffy pilau and biriani.

Tamarind

This sour fruit is available dried, pressed into blocks or sold as a purée in jars. The liquid version is generally less sour, so add up to twice what the recipe calls for but, as always, be guided by taste.

Tandoori mix

A blend of hot and fragrant spices including cardamom, chilli, turmeric, saffron and garam masala. If commercial brands are not available, substitute the following: 2 teaspoons ground turmeric, 1 teaspoon paprika, ½ teaspoon chilli powder (optional), 1 teaspoon garam masala (page 19), ½ teaspoon ground cardamom, ⅛ teaspoon powdered saffron. You may also add ½ teaspoon of garlic powder, but this is not necessary if fresh garlic is used in the recipe.

Yoghurt

In India this is called *dahi*, or curd, and is always unflavoured. Plain yoghurt should be used, and if possible choose one with a definite sour flavour. I have found that goat's milk yoghurt or Greek-style yoghurt is most suitable.

Curry powders and pastes

Curry powder, as it is sold commercially, is almost never used in India or other countries where curry is made and eaten every day. Rather, the individual spices are freshly ground each day and added to the food in various combinations and proportions. Even when there is a grinding mill in the town and home cooks, yielding to the pressures of modern living, have a month's supply ground at a time, the dry ground spices are kept separate.

There are many good curry mixtures sold commercially, but there are also many that lack good flavour because of a skimping on the more expensive spices and a reliance on 'fillers', such as rice flour, to make up the bulk. If using curry powder, make sure it is fresh by buying from a store that specialises in spices with a high turnover, buy in small quantities so it does not stay on your shelf for too long and look for a brand in a bottle or tin, because cardboard containers absorb a lot of the essential oils of the spices.

In most of the recipes in this book I have used the individual spices to allow for as much variation as possible. Spicing is an art you can learn, and eventually you can tailor your curries to your own taste and not rely on a ready-mixed formula. However, if you cannot obtain the spices mentioned or have a liking for a particular curry mixture, substitute a similar quantity of the blend for the combined amount of turmeric, coriander, cumin, chilli, fennel and fenugreek used in the recipe. Curry powder does not include the fragrant spices such as cardamom, clove and cinnamon, so these must be added separately. A curry paste I like to buy or make is green masala paste, based on fresh herbs. Because these are not always in season it is a good idea to make a batch when they are plentiful and preserve them in oil for later use (see page 21). It can take the place of fresh ginger and coriander (cilantro) leaves and even part of the garlic in a recipe, or it can be used as an extra flavour accent.

Another important ingredient is garam masala, a mixture of ground spices, which is added to many types of Indian dishes. Sometimes it is added with other spices at the frying stage, but more often it is sprinkled on during the last few minutes of cooking.

Your Indian And Pakistani Shelf

These ingredients will put an entire range of Indian spice dishes at your fingertips. Fresh ingredients are not included, only those that have a good shelf life. Buy in small quantities and store in airtight jars away from heat and direct sunlight.

amchur powder (glossary)

asafoetida (glossary)

besan (chickpea flour)

black cumin seeds

black mustard seeds

black peppercorns, whole and ground

cardamom, whole pods and ground

chilli powder

cinnamon sticks

cloves, whole and ground

coconut, desiccated (shredded)

coconut milk (pages 6–8)

coriander, seeds and ground

cumin, seeds and ground

curry leaves

curry pastes (page 16)

fennel, seeds and ground

fenugreek, seeds and ground

garam masala (page 19)

ghee

kencur (aromatic ginger) powder (glossary)

kewra essence (glossary)

mace, ground

nigella seeds

nutmeg, whole

panch phora (page 15)

rosewater

saffron, strands or ground

tandoori mix (page 16)

turmeric, ground

Curry
Powders
and
Pastes

✹

Garam Masala

The recipes that follow will give you a good selection to choose from to suit your own personal taste. Roasting the spices brings out their flavour and also makes them easier to grind. If a spice grinder is not available, use a blender or mortar and pestle to pound the spices to a fine powder (when the spices are still warm and crisp after roasting this process is made much easier). Store garam masala in an airtight jar in a cool, dark place for up to 6 months. Freezing may help preserve the essential oils.

No. 1 Garam masala

25 g (1 oz) coriander seeds

2 tablespoons cumin seeds

1 tablespoon whole black peppercorns

20 g (¾ oz/¼ cup) cardamom pods

4 cinnamon sticks

1 teaspoon whole cloves

1 whole nutmeg, finely grated

Roast the coriander seeds in a small frying pan over low heat. As it starts to smell fragrant, remove it to a plate. Repeat with the cumin seeds, peppercorns, cardamom pods, cinnamon sticks and cloves, cooking separately until all are fragrant.

After roasting, peel the cardamom pods, discarding the pods. Place the cardamom seeds in a spice grinder with the other roasted spices and blend to a fine powder. Stir in the nutmeg to combine. Store in an airtight jar.

No. 2 Fragrant spice garam masala

3 cinnamon sticks

20 g (¾ oz/¼ cup) cardamom pods

1 teaspoon whole cloves

1 teaspoon ground mace or ½ teaspoon
  freshly grated nutmeg

Roast the cinnamon sticks in a small frying pan over low heat. As it starts to smell fragrant, remove to a plate. Repeat with the cardamom pods, cloves and mace, if using, cooking separately until all are fragrant.

After roasting, peel the cardamom pods, discarding the pods. Place the cardamom seeds in a spice grinder with the other roasted spices and blend to a fine powder. Stir in the nutmeg, if using. Store in an airtight jar.

No. 3 Kashmiri garam masala

2 cinnamon sticks

20 g (¾ oz/¼ cup) cardamom pods

½ teaspoon whole cloves

1 teaspoon black cumin seeds

1 teaspoon whole black peppercorns

whole nutmeg, finely grated

Roast the cinnamon stick in a small frying pan over low heat. As it starts to smell fragrant, remove it to a plate. Repeat with the cardamom pods, cloves, cumin seeds and peppercorns, cooking separately until all are fragrant.

After roasting, peel the cardamom pods, discarding the pods. Place the cardamom seeds in a spice grinder with the other roasted spices and blend to a fine powder. Stir in the nutmeg. Store in an airtight jar.

Madrasi Masala
Madras–style curry paste

100 g (3½ oz/1 cup) ground coriander

50 g (1¾ oz/½ cup) ground cumin

1 tablespoon ground turmeric

1 tablespoon black mustard seeds, ground

1 tablespoon chilli powder

1 tablespoon freshly ground black pepper

1 tablespoon salt

2 tablespoons crushed garlic

2 tablespoons finely grated fresh ginger

vinegar for mixing

190 ml (6½ fl oz/¾ cup) vegetable oil

Combine the ground spices and salt in a bowl. Add the garlic and ginger and just enough vinegar to make a smooth, thick purée.

Heat the oil in a saucepan over high heat. When the oil is hot, add the spice mixture, then reduce the heat and stir constantly until the spices are cooked and the oil starts to separate. Remove from the heat and allow to cool. Store in an airtight jar in the refrigerator for up to 3 months.

Use about 1 tablespoon curry paste for each 500 g (1 lb 2 oz) of meat, fish or poultry, substituting it for the garlic, ginger and spices in a recipe.

Taaza Masala
Green masala paste

A spice paste based on fresh coriander (cilantro) leaves, mint, garlic and ginger. Added to any curry or spiced preparation, it will give extra flavour.

1 teaspoon fenugreek seeds

5 large garlic cloves

2 tablespoons finely grated fresh ginger

20 g (¾ oz/1 cup) firmly packed fresh mint leaves

30 g (1 oz/1 cup) firmly packed fresh coriander (cilantro) leaves

125 ml (4 fl oz/½ cup) vinegar

3 teaspoons salt

2 teaspoons ground turmeric

½ teaspoon ground cloves

1 teaspoon ground cardamom

125 ml (4 fl oz/½ cup) vegetable oil

60 ml (2 fl oz/¼ cup) sesame oil

Put the fenugreek seeds in a bowl of water and leave to soak overnight – they will swell and develop a jelly-like coating.

Measure 1 teaspoon of the soaked seeds and place in a food processor or blender with the garlic, ginger, mint, coriander and vinegar. Process until well combined and very smooth. Add the salt, turmeric, cloves and cardamom and stir to combine.

Heat the vegetable and sesame oils in a saucepan over high heat. When the oil is hot, add the spice mixture and bring to the boil. Remove from the heat and allow to cool. Transfer to an airtight jar – the oil should cover the herbs; if it doesn't, heat a little extra oil and add it to the jar. The curry paste can be stored in the refrigerator for up to 3 months.

Curry Powders and Pastes

Breads

✳

Chapatis
Wholemeal unleavened pan-fried bread

Makes: 20–24

These flat discs of unleavened bread have a delightful flavour and chewy texture. They can be served simply with butter, alongside dry curries or vegetable dishes.

Chapati dough

370 g (13 oz/2 cups) wholemeal (whole-wheat) atta or roti flour, plus extra for dusting

1–1½ teaspoons salt, or to taste

1 tablespoon ghee or oil (optional)

Note

In India, chapatis are cooked on the tawa or griddle plate and are held for a moment or two right over the fire – this makes them puff up like balloons. You can do this over a gas flame, holding them with kitchen tongs.

To make the chapati dough, put the flour and salt in a mixing bowl and rub in the ghee, if using. Add 250 ml (8½ fl oz/1 cup) water and mix to a firm but not stiff dough. Continue to knead for at least 10 minutes (the more it is kneaded, the lighter the bread will be). Form the dough into a ball, cover with plastic wrap and stand for at least 1 hour or longer. (If left overnight the chapatis will be very light and tender.)

Shape the dough into balls with a 5 cm (2 in) diameter. Roll out each ball on a lightly floured work surface to make a thin circle – you should have about 20 rounds.

Heat a griddle plate or a large heavy-based frying pan over high heat. Start cooking the chapatis with those that were rolled first (the resting between rolling and cooking also seems to make for lighter chapatis). Cook for about 1 minute, then turn and cook for a further 1 minute, pressing lightly around the edges of the chapati with a folded tea towel (dish towel) or a spatula – this encourages bubbles to form and makes the chapatis light. As each one is cooked, wrap in a clean tea towel until all are cooked. Serve immediately.

Dal Chapati
Chapatis with lentil and spinach filling

Makes: 8

1 quantity chapati dough (page 23)

250 g (9 oz/1 cup) red lentils

195 g (7 oz/3 cups) finely chopped
    English spinach

2 tablespoons oil or ghee, plus
    1 tablespoon extra

1 onion, finely chopped

1 garlic clove, finely chopped

1 teaspoon ground cumin

½ teaspoon garam masala (page 19)

1 teaspoon salt, or to taste

a squeeze of lemon juice

Make the chapati dough as directed on page 23 but add an extra generous measure of water to make a softer, more pliable dough. Knead well and set aside.

To make the filling, put the lentils into a saucepan and add enough water to cover by 1.5 cm (½ in). Bring to the boil, then reduce the heat to low, cover, and simmer for 5 minutes, then stir in the spinach and cook for a further 5 minutes, or until the lentils are tender – you may need to add more water.

Heat the ghee in a frying pan over medium heat. Cook the onion until soft and golden, then add the garlic and lentil and spinach mixture and stir to combine. Add the cumin, garam masala, salt and lemon juice and continue to cook, stirring regularly, until all the liquid has been absorbed and the mixture is dry. Remove from the heat and allow to cool; taste and adjust the seasoning.

Divide the chapati dough into 8 even-sized balls and press them to make circles with a 10 cm (4 in) diameter. Put a spoonful of the lentil and spinach mixture into the centre of each, then bring the edges of the dough together and pinch well to seal. Roll each chapati out into circles with a 20 cm (8 in) diameter on a lightly floured work surface – they should be thin, but not so thin that the dough breaks and lets the filling out.

Heat a little ghee on a griddle plate or in a large heavy-based frying pan over high heat. Cook the chapatis, in batches, pressing gently until golden on the underside. Brush a little extra ghee over the top of each, then turn and cook until golden. Remove to a plate and cover with a clean tea towel (dish towel) while cooking the remainder. Serve hot.

Puri
Deep-fried wholemeal bread

Makes: about 20

1 quantity chapati dough (page 23)

oil for deep-frying

Make the chapati dough as directed on page 23. Shape the dough into balls with a 5 cm (2 in) diameter. Roll out each ball on a lightly floured work surface to make a thin circle – you should have about 20 rounds.

Heat the oil in a large heavy-based saucepan over medium heat. When the oil is hot, deep-fry the puris, one at a time, spooning the hot oil over the top continually until it puffs and swells. Turn over and cook the other side. When pale golden brown, drain on paper towel. Repeat until all are cooked. Serve warm with curries and *bhajis*.

Kachori
Puris with filling

Makes: about 20

1 quantity chapati dough (page 23)

235 g (8½ oz/1 cup) Potato and pea dry curry (page 136) or Dal (page 134), mashed

oil for deep-frying

Make the chapati dough as directed on page 23. Shape the dough into balls with a 5 cm (2 in) diameter. Roll out each ball on a lightly floured work surface to make a thin circle – you should have about 20 rounds.

Put a spoonful of the curry into the centre of each circle, then bring the edges of the dough together and pinch well to seal. Roll each puri out on a lightly floured work surface – they should be thin, but not so thin that the dough breaks and lets the filling out.

Heat the oil in a large heavy-based saucepan over medium heat. When the oil is hot, deep-fry the puris, one at a time, spooning the hot oil over the top continually until it puffs and swells. Turn over and cook the other side. When pale golden brown, drain on paper towel. Repeat until all are cooked.

Alu Puri
Potato puris

Makes: 20–24

---

230 g (8 oz/1 cup) mashed potato, cooled

300 g (10½ oz/2 cups) plain (all-purpose) flour

2 teaspoons salt

oil for deep-frying

1 tablespoon ghee (optional)

Mix together the mashed potato, flour and salt in a bowl. Knead well, adding about 60 ml (2 fl oz/¼ cup) lukewarm water to make a firm but not dry dough. The more the dough is kneaded, the lighter the puris will be, so knead for at least 10 minutes, or until the dough is smooth and not sticky. Cover and rest for 30–60 minutes.

Divide the potato mixture into 20–24 even-sized balls, and roll each one out on a lightly floured work surface to make circles with a 10 cm (4 in) diameter.

Heat the oil and ghee in a large heavy-based saucepan over medium heat. When the oil is hot, deep-fry the puris, one at a time, spooning the hot oil over the top continually until it puffs and swells. Turn over and cook the other side. When pale golden brown, drain on paper towel. Repeat until all are cooked. Serve warm with lentils, vegetables or meat curries that do not have a lot of thin gravy.

Paratha
Flaky wholemeal bread

Makes: 12–14

Probably the favourite variety of Indian bread, parathas are rich, flaky and deliciously flavoured with ghee. Kebabs and parathas is a combination which is quite famous. A dear friend of my grandmother taught me her method of rolling and folding the parathas, which is the easiest and most successful I've tried.

225 g (8 oz/1½ cups) wholemeal (whole-wheat) flour

225 g (8 oz/1½ cups) plain (all-purpose) flour or roti flour

1½ teaspoons salt

120–160 g (4½–5½ oz) ghee, melted, plus extra for cooking

Note

The wholemeal and plain or roti flour can be replaced by 450 g (1 lb/3 cups) plain (all-purpose) flour if necessary.

Sift the wholemeal flour, plain flour and salt into a mixing bowl and rub in 1 tablespoon of the ghee. Add 250 ml (8½ fl oz/1 cup) water and mix to a firm but not stiff dough. Continue kneading for at least 10 minutes (the more it is kneaded, the lighter the bread will be). Form the dough into a ball, cover and rest for at least 1 hour.

Divide the dough into 12–14 equal portions and roll to make smooth balls. Roll out each ball on a lightly floured work surface to make a very thin circular shape. Pour 2 teaspoons of the melted ghee into the centre of each and spread lightly with your hand. With a knife, make a cut from the centre of each circle to the outer edge. Starting at the cut edge, roll the dough closely into a cone shape. Pick it up, press the apex of the cone and the base towards each other and flatten slightly. You will now have a small, roughly circular lump of dough again.

Roll out each portion again on a lightly floured surface, taking care not to press too hard and let the air out at the edges. The parathas should be as round as possible, but not too thin.

Heat a little extra ghee on a griddle plate or in a large heavy-based frying pan over high heat. Cook the parathas, in batches, brushing over more ghee, until they are golden brown on both sides. Serve hot with grilled kebabs, sambals and *podina chatni*.

Gobi Paratha
Parathas with cauliflower filling

Makes: 8

300 g (10½ oz/2 cups) roti flour or plain
(all-purpose) flour

½ teaspoon salt

40–60 g (1½–2 oz) ghee, melted

Filling

125 g (4½ oz/1 cup) cauliflower florets,
finely chopped

2 teaspoons finely grated fresh ginger

1 teaspoon salt

1 teaspoon garam masala (page 19)

chilli powder to taste (optional)

Mix the flour and salt together in a large bowl, then add 170 ml (5½ fl oz/⅔ cup) lukewarm water all at once and knead hard for 10 minutes to make a firm but pliable dough. Cover and rest for at least 30 minutes.

To make the filling, combine all the ingredients in a bowl and mix well. Use only the tender flower heads of the cauliflower and make sure there are no large pieces, as these will make the parathas difficult to roll out.

Divide the dough into 8 even-sized portions and roll each into a ball. Press each out to make a circle with a 10 cm (4 in) diameter. Put a spoonful of the filling into the centre of each, then bring the edges of the dough together and pinch well to seal. Press with your hands to flatten, then roll each paratha out on a lightly floured work surface – they should be thin, but not so thin that the dough breaks and lets the filling out. Do not press too hard on the rolling pin or the filling will break through the dough. If this does happen take a small piece of dough, press flat and place it over the break. Roll gently to join.

Heat a little of the ghee on a griddle plate or in a large heavy-based frying pan over high heat. Cook the parathas, one at a time, spreading a little ghee over the top of each before turning and cooking to golden on both sides. Serve at once, accompanied by a raita.

Breads ✦

Naan
Punjabi leavened bread

Makes: about 8 loaves

30 g (1 oz) fresh compressed yeast or
  2 teaspoons dried yeast

3 teaspoons sugar

60 g (2½ oz/¼ cup) plain yoghurt

1 egg, beaten

60 ml (2 fl oz/¼ cup) melted ghee or butter,
  plus extra for brushing

2 teaspoons salt

525 g (1 lb 3 oz/3½ cups) plain (all-purpose)
  flour

2 tablespoons poppy seeds or nigella seeds

Put the yeast and 60 ml (2 fl oz/¼ cup) lukewarm water in a small bowl and leave for a few minutes to soften, then stir to dissolve. Add 1 teaspoon of the sugar, stir, then leave in a warm place for 10 minutes, or until the mixture starts to froth. This is to test whether the yeast is live; if it does not froth start again with a fresh batch of yeast.

Stir the yoghurt in a bowl until smooth, then add the remaining sugar, 125 ml (4 fl oz/½ cup) lukewarm water, the egg, ghee and salt. Stir in the yeast mixture.

Put 300 g (10½ oz/2 cups) of the flour into a mixing bowl and make a well in the centre. Pour in the yeast mixture, beating well with a wooden spoon to make a smooth batter. Add the remaining flour a little at a time and when it gets too stiff to use the spoon, knead with your hands until a firm dough forms. Continue kneading for 10–12 minutes, or until the dough is smooth and elastic, using as little extra flour as possible.

Form the dough into a ball and set aside. Heat a bowl by running warm water into it and leaving for a few minutes.

Dry the bowl well, grease it with the extra ghee, then place the dough in the bowl and turn to coat. Cover with a clean tea towel (dish towel) and leave in a warm place until doubled in size and a finger pushed into the dough leaves an impression.

Preheat the oven to 230°C (445°F). Put 2 ungreased baking trays into the oven to preheat.

Knock back the dough and divide it into 8 even-sized portions; leave to rest for 10 minutes. Pat the dough into circles, keeping them thin in the centre and thicker around the rim, then pull one end outwards, making a teardrop shape. They should be a handspan long and little more than half that much wide at the base. Brush with the extra melted ghee and sprinkle over the poppy seeds. Bake on the preheated trays in the oven for 10 minutes, or until golden and puffed. If the naan are not brown enough, finish off under a preheated grill (broiler) for 1–2 minutes.

Serve warm or cool with tandoori chicken, Lamb kebabs, Korma or Botee kebab, and with Kachumbar as an accompaniment.

Rice

*

Namkin Chawal

Plain savoury rice

Serves: 2–4

Rice is the staple food in southern, central and eastern parts of India and forms the major part of an Indian meal. Served Indian-style, this quantity will serve two.

50 g (1¾ oz/¼ cup) long-grain rice

10 g (¼ oz) ghee

1 teaspoon salt

Wash the rice well and drain in a colander for 30 minutes.

Heat the ghee in a heavy-based saucepan. Add the rice and stir for about 2 minutes, then add the salt and 625 ml (21 fl oz/2½ cups) hot water and bring to the boil. Reduce the heat to low, cover, and cook without lifting the lid or stirring, for 20–25 minutes. Lift the lid to allow the steam to escape for a minute or two, then use a fork to lightly fluff up the rice, taking care not to mash the grains, which should be firm and separate and perfectly cooked.

Serve the rice using a slotted spoon rather than a wooden spoon, which will crush the grains. Serve with curries or other spiced dishes.

Rice ✦

Kitchri

Savoury rice and lentils

Serves: 4–6

200 g (7 oz/1 cup) long-grain rice

250 g (9 oz/1 cup) red lentils

50 g (1¾ oz) ghee

2 onions, thinly sliced

2½ teaspoons salt

1½ teaspoons garam masala (page 19)

Wash the rice well and drain in a colander for 30 minutes. Wash the lentils well, removing any that float to the surface, then drain.

Heat the ghee in a heavy-based saucepan. Add the onion and cook over medium heat until golden brown. Remove half the onion to a plate. Add the rice and lentils to the pan and cook for about 3 minutes, stirring constantly. Add 1.25 litres (42 fl oz/5 cups) hot water, the salt and garam masala and stir to combine. Bring to the boil, then reduce the heat, cover, and simmer over low heat for 20–25 minutes, or until the rice and lentils are tender. Do not lift the lid or stir during cooking. Serve hot, garnished with the reserved fried onion.

Note

This is a soft kitchri with the consistency of porridge. If a drier, fluffier result is desired, reduce the water to 875 ml (29½ fl oz/3 cups). Also, whole spices, such as a cinnamon stick and a few whole cloves, bruised cardamom pods and peppercorns may be used instead of garam masala.

Parsi Pilau
Spiced rice, Parsi-style

Serves: 5–6

450 g (1 lb/2½ cups) long-grain rice

½ teaspoon saffron strands

1 tablespoon boiling water

40 g (1½ oz) ghee

4 cardamom pods, bruised

1 small cinnamon stick

4 whole cloves

10 whole black peppercorns

2½ teaspoons salt

finely grated zest of 1 orange

2 tablespoons sultanas (golden raisins)

2 tablespoons sliced almonds

2 tablespoons pistachio nuts

Wash the rice well and drain in a colander for 30 minutes.

Gently heat the saffron strands in a small frying pan over low heat for 1–2 minutes, shaking the pan frequently and making sure they don't burn. Remove to a plate to cool and crisp, then crush to a powder in a cup, adding the boiling water and stirring to dissolve. Set aside.

Heat the ghee in a heavy-based saucepan. Add the cardamom pods, cinnamon stick, cloves and peppercorns and cook for 2 minutes, or until aromatic. Add the rice and continue stirring for 2–3 minutes, then add 1 litre (34 fl oz/4 cups) hot water, the salt, orange zest and saffron water, stirring well to combine. Bring to the boil, then reduce the heat to low, cover, and simmer for 20 minutes, or until all the liquid has been absorbed. Scatter the sultanas over the rice, replace the lid and continue cooking for a further 5 minutes.

Serve the rice garnished with almonds and pistachio nuts. This is very good served with Dhansak, a famous Parsi dish of meat or chicken cooked with lentils and vegetables (page 94).

Kesar Pilau
Saffron and lemon sweet pilau

Serves: 4–6

The very best way to get a uniform colour and maximum flavour from saffron is to toast the strands in a dry frying pan over low heat for 1–2 minutes, shaking the pan frequently so the saffron doesn't burn. Remove to a plate to cool and crisp, then they are easy to crush to a powder in a cup with the back of a spoon. Add a tablespoon of hot water to dissolve the powder. If you want the rice evenly coloured, use this method. For a more speckled effect, use the soaking method described in this recipe.

20 g (¾ oz) ghee

6 cardamom pods, bruised

4 whole cloves

1 small cinnamon stick

250 g (9 oz/1¼ cups) long-grain rice

60 ml (2 fl oz/¼ cup) lemon juice

1 tablespoon sugar

1 teaspoon salt

¼ teaspoon saffron strands

2 tablespoons boiling water

Heat the ghee in a heavy-based saucepan over low heat. Add the cardamom pods, cloves and cinnamon stick and cook for 3 minutes. Add the rice and cook for about 4–5 minutes, then add 500 ml (17 fl oz/2 cups) hot water, the lemon juice, sugar and salt, stirring well. Bring to the boil, then reduce the heat to low, cover, and cook for 10 minutes.

Meanwhile, put the saffron strands in a small bowl and pour over the boiling water; leave to soak for 5 minutes. Press the strands between your fingers to extract as much colour as possible. After 10 minutes, sprinkle the saffron water into the pan over the rice. Do not stir. Replace the lid and cook for a further 10 minutes. Uncover, to allow the steam to escape for a few minutes, then remove the whole spices. Use a fork to gently fluff the rice grains before serving.

Mattar Pilau
Rice with fresh green peas

Serves: 2–3

1 tablespoon ghee or oil

4 whole cloves

1 small cinnamon stick

2 cardamom pods

1 teaspoon cumin seeds

½ teaspoon ground turmeric (optional)

250 g (9 oz/1¼ cups) long-grain rice

195 g (7 oz/1¼ cups) fresh or frozen peas

2 teaspoons salt

Heat the ghee in a heavy-based saucepan over medium heat. Add the cloves, cinnamon stick, cardamom pods and cumin seeds and cook for 1 minute. Add the turmeric and rice and cook for 2 minutes, stirring constantly. Add the fresh peas, if using, the salt and 625 ml (21 fl oz/2½ cups) hot water and bring to the boil, then reduce the heat to low, cover, and cook for 25 minutes without lifting the lid or stirring. Remove the whole spices and use a fork to fluff up the grains before serving. Serve hot with vegetable or meat dishes.

Note

If using frozen peas, quickly lift the lid and scatter over the rice 10 minutes before the end of cooking time.

Sabzi Pilau
Rice with vegetables

Serves: 5–6

40 g (1½ oz) ghee

2 tablespoons oil

2 onions, thinly sliced

1 garlic clove, finely chopped

400 g (14 oz/2 cups) long-grain rice

2 teaspoons salt, plus extra to taste

1 teaspoon garam masala (page 19)

2 carrots, cut into thin matchsticks

12 green beans, thinly sliced

80 g (2¾ oz/½ cup) diced red or green capsicum (bell pepper)

1 small potato, peeled and cubed

80 g (2¾ oz/½ cup) fresh or frozen peas

Heat the ghee and oil in a large heavy-based saucepan over low heat. Add the onion and cook for 10 minutes, or until soft and pale golden. Add the garlic and continue cooking for 2 minutes, then add the rice. Increase the heat to medium and cook for 2 minutes, then add 1 litre (34 fl oz/4 cups) hot water, the salt and garam masala. Bring to the boil, then reduce the heat to low, cover, and cook for 15 minutes, or until all the liquid has been absorbed.

Add the carrot, beans, capsicum, potato and peas to the pan – do not stir. Sprinkle with a little extra salt to taste. Replace the lid and cook for a further 10 minutes, or until the vegetables are tender but not overcooked. Uncover the pan and leave for a few minutes, then use a fork to fluff up the grains and combine the vegetables. Use a slotted metal spoon to serve with curries.

Note

You can garnish this dish with fried almonds and sultanas (golden raisins) if you like.

Jhinga Pilau
Spiced prawns and rice

Serves: 4

300 g (10½ oz/1½ cups) long-grain rice

40 g (1½ oz) ghee

2 tablespoons oil

500 g (1 lb 2 oz) raw prawns (shrimp),
   peeled and deveined

1 onion, thinly sliced

3 garlic cloves, crushed

½ teaspoon finely grated fresh ginger

4 cardamom pods, bruised

4 whole cloves

1 small cinnamon stick

1 teaspoon garam masala (page 19)

2 fresh red chillies, sliced

½ teaspoon chilli powder (optional)

1½ teaspoons salt

thinly sliced cucumber to garnish

fresh coriander (cilantro) leaves to garnish

Wash the rice well and drain in a colander for 30 minutes.

Heat the ghee and oil in a large heavy-based saucepan over medium–high heat. Add the prawns and cook until they change colour, then remove to a plate.

Add the onion, garlic and ginger and cook for a few minutes, stirring frequently. Add the whole spices and cook for about 1–2 minutes further, then add the rice and stir to coat.

Return the prawns to the pan and add the garam masala, chilli, chilli powder, salt and 750 ml (2½ fl oz/3 cups) hot water.

Bring to the boil, then reduce the heat to low, cover, and cook for 20 minutes without lifting the lid. Serve hot, garnished with cucumber and fresh coriander.

Yakhni Pilau
Rice cooked in stock with spices

Serves: 4–6

1 kg (2 lb 3 oz) whole chicken or use
   3 lamb shanks

4 cardamom pods

10 whole black peppercorns

4½ teaspoons salt

1 onion

3 whole cloves

500 g (1 lb 2 oz/2½ cups) long-grain or
   basmati rice

120 g (4½ oz) ghee

1 large onion, thinly sliced

¼ teaspoon saffron strands or ½ teaspoon
   ground saffron

2 garlic cloves, crushed

½ teaspoon finely grated fresh ginger

½ teaspoon garam masala (page 19)

½ teaspoon ground cardamom

60 ml (2 fl oz/¼ cup) rosewater

30 g (1 oz/¼ cup) sultanas (golden raisins)

40 g (1½ oz/¼ cup) almonds, toasted

155 g (5½ oz/1 cup) cooked green peas

3 hard-boiled eggs, halved

Make a stock by putting the chicken or lamb shanks in a large saucepan and enough water to cover, with the cardamom pods, peppercorns, 2 teaspoons of the salt and the onion stuck with the cloves. Bring to the boil, then reduce the heat to low and simmer for 2 hours. Strain the stock, reserving 1 litre (34 fl oz/4 cups) for the rice, and cool. Remove the meat from the bones, cut into bite-sized pieces and set aside.

Wash the rice well and drain in a colander for 30 minutes. Heat the ghee in a large heavy-based saucepan and cook the onion until golden. Add the saffron, garlic and ginger and cook for 1 minute, stirring constantly. Add the rice and stir with a slotted spoon for 5 minutes over medium heat – this prevents the delicate rice grains breaking. Add the reserved hot stock, garam masala, cardamom, remaining salt, rosewater, sultanas and reserved meat and stir well, then cover and cook over low heat for 20 minutes, or until tender – do not uncover the pan or stir the rice. Remove from the heat and use a fork to fluff up the rice. Garnish with the almonds, peas and eggs. This dish can be served with pickles, Cucumbers in spiced yoghurt (page 155) or sour cream, and crisp fried pappadams. A curry dish can also be served.

Moglai Biriani
Moghul biriani

Serves: 12–14

Biriani is a very rich pilau, usually layered with a spicy mutton or chicken savoury mixture and steamed very gently so that the flavours blend. It is the masterpiece of many Eastern cooks and the central dish at festive dinners. Here is a recipe for a lamb biriani, suitable for serving at a party. Halve all quantities for a smaller number of people; cooking times stay the same.

Lamb savoury

2 kg (4 lb 6 oz) boned leg of lamb, trimmed of fat

100 g (3½ oz) ghee

3 large onions, sliced

6 garlic cloves, chopped

1½ tablespoons finely chopped fresh ginger

120 g (4½ oz) Indian curry powder

1 tablespoon salt

2 tablespoons lemon juice

1 teaspoon garam masala (page 19)

1 teaspoon ground cardamom

2 fresh red chillies, left whole

25 g (1 oz/½ cup) chopped fresh mint

4 ripe tomatoes, peeled and chopped

3 tablespoons chopped fresh coriander (cilantro) leaves to garnish

2 quantities Yakhni pilau (page 41), using lamb shanks

20 g (¾ oz) ghee

To make the lamb savoury, cut the lamb into large cubes. Heat the ghee in a saucepan over medium heat. Add the onion, garlic and ginger and cook until soft and golden. Add the curry powder and cook for 1 minute further, then add the salt, lemon juice and lamb and cook, stirring constantly, until it is well coated in the spice mixture. Add the garam masala, cardamom, whole chillies, mint and tomato. Cover and cook over low heat for approximately 1 hour, stirring occasionally, until the lamb is tender and the gravy is very thick and almost dry. Remove from the heat and remove and discard the chillies. Sprinkle with the chopped coriander leaves.

To make the yakhni pilau follow the directions on page 41 using lamb shanks to make the stock – although you are doubling the ingredients the cooking times are the same. When the pilau is cooked, allow to cool slightly.

Preheat the oven to 160°C (320°F). To assemble the biriani, heat the ghee in a large ovenproof casserole and spoon in one-third of the pilau, packing it lightly. Spread half of the lamb savoury over the top, making sure it goes right to the edges of the casserole. Cover with half of the remaining pilau. Repeat this layering to finish with a layer of pilau. Cover the casserole and cook in the oven for 20–30 minutes. Leave the biriani in the dish or turn out onto a large serving tray. Garnish as for the yakhni pilau.

Note

For special occasions add blanched pistachio nuts and edible silver leaf to the garnish in traditional Indian style.

Savouries
and Snacks

✦

Channa Ki Dal
Savoury split peas

Serves: 10

Serve these as a tasty nibble with drinks, or store them in an airtight container for a snack any time.

440 g (14 oz/2 cups) yellow split peas

1 tablespoon bicarbonate of soda
 (baking soda)

oil for deep-frying

1 teaspoon garam masala (page 19)

½ teaspoon chilli powder (optional)

2 teaspoons salt

½ teaspoon amchur powder (optional)

Wash the split peas well two or three times. Dissolve the bicarbonate of soda in a bowl of fresh cold water, add the split peas and leave to soak for at least 12 hours or overnight. Rinse in fresh water and drain again, first in a colander and then on paper towel, until the split peas are dry.

Heat the oil in a large heavy-based saucepan over medium heat. When the oil is hot, deep-fry the split peas, in batches, until golden. (Make sure the oil is not so hot that it burns the peas; if it is not hot enough they will be very oily.)

Remove the peas from the pan with a mesh skimmer and drain on paper towel. When all the peas are cooked and drained, make a mixture of the spices and salt and toss the peas in it. Allow to cool before serving. The savoury split peas can be stored in an airtight container for up to 10 days.

Channa
Savoury chickpeas

Serves: 4–6

275 g (9½ oz/1¼ cups) dried chickpeas
 (garbanzo beans)

2 teaspoons salt, plus extra to taste

1 teaspoon ground turmeric

1 teaspoon ground cumin

½ teaspoon chilli powder

lemon juice to taste

Soak the chickpeas overnight in a bowl with plenty of water. Next day, transfer to a saucepan, pour in enough fresh water to cover, add the salt and turmeric. Bring to the boil, then reduce the heat to low, cover, and simmer for 35–45 minutes, or until the chickpeas are tender. Drain and transfer to a bowl.

Sprinkle the cumin and chilli powder over the chickpeas and add lemon juice and salt, to taste. Toss well to coat and serve the chickpeas as a snack by themselves, or as part of the Pani puri accompaniments (page 54).

Masala Kaju Badam
Spicy fried nuts

Serves: 20

255 g (9 oz/1⅔ cups) raw cashew nuts

255 g (9 oz/1⅔ cups) blanched almonds

560 g (1 lb 4 oz/3½ cups) raw peanuts

oil for frying

1 tablespoon salt

2 teaspoons garam masala (page 19)

2 teaspoons chilli powder, or to taste

1 teaspoon amchur powder (optional)

Heat the oil in a large heavy-based frying pan over medium heat and cook all the nuts until golden. Remove with a slotted spoon and drain on paper towel. (Do not leave them in the oil until they darken because they go on cooking in their own heat.) Combine the salt and spices and sprinkle over the nuts. If an acid flavour is liked, add amchur powder to the mix. Cool, then store in an airtight container for up to 2 weeks.

Sev or Murukku
Deep-fried lentil savoury

Serves: 12

165 g (6 oz/1½ cups) besan (chickpea flour)

125 g (4½ oz/¾ cup) ground rice

1½ teaspoons garam masala (page 19)

½ teaspoon chilli powder (optional)

½ teaspoon ajowan seeds (optional)

½ teaspoon cumin seeds

1½ teaspoons salt, or to taste

60 g (2 oz) ghee, melted

oil for deep-frying

Sift the besan into a large bowl and stir through the ground rice, spices, aromatic seeds and salt. Rub in the ghee until evenly distributed. Add 170 ml (5½ fl oz/⅔ cup) water and knead to a stiff dough – it should resemble the consistency of a piped biscuit (cookie) dough.

Heat the oil in a large heavy-based saucepan over medium heat. Put some of the dough into a potato ricer or mouli grater and push through into the hot oil, and deep-fry until golden brown. Lift out with a mesh skimmer and drain on paper towel. Repeat until all the dough has been used. Cool, then store in an airtight container for up to 2 weeks. You can sprinkle over a little extra spice and salt after cooking if you prefer.

Alu Lachche
Potato straws

Serves: 8

4 large potatoes

ice-cold water for soaking

oil for deep-frying

1 teaspoon salt

½ teaspoon chilli powder

½ teaspoon ground cumin

½ teaspoon garam masala (page 19)

Peel the potatoes and cut into thin matchsticks. Soak in ice-cold water, then drain and dry well on paper towel.

Heat the oil in a large heavy-based saucepan over medium heat. When the oil is hot, deep-fry the potato straws, one handful at a time, until they are crisp and golden. Lift out of the oil with a slotted spoon and drain well on paper towel.

When all the potato is cooked, sprinkle over the combined salt and spices and toss to coat before serving.

Alu Chat
Potato slices

Serves: 8

6–8 small potatoes

1 teaspoon salt

1 teaspoon ground cumin

½ teaspoon chilli powder

½ teaspoon garam masala (page 19)

1 tablespoon lemon juice

Wash the potatoes and cook them in their skins in a saucepan of boiling water – do not overcook. Drain, then allow to cool a little before peeling and cutting them into slices. Combine the salt and ground spices and sprinkle them over the top. Add the lemon juice and toss lightly to combine. Serve hot, as a snack.

Samoosa
Small savoury pastries

Makes: 32–36

These popular savouries are served for afternoon tea in India, but they are equally suitable served with pre-dinner drinks.

Samoosa pastry

225 g (8 oz/1½ cups) plain (all-purpose) flour

¾ teaspoon salt

1 tablespoon oil or ghee

Savoury mince filling

1 tablespoon oil or ghee, plus extra for deep-frying

1 garlic clove, finely chopped

1 teaspoon finely chopped fresh ginger

2 onions, finely chopped

2 teaspoons curry powder

½ teaspoon salt

1 tablespoon vinegar or lemon juice

250 g (9 oz) minced (ground) beef or lamb

1 teaspoon garam masala (page 19)

2 tablespoons chopped fresh mint or coriander (cilantro) leaves

oil for deep-frying

To make the pastry, sift the flour and salt into a bowl, then add the oil and 125 ml (4 fl oz/½ cup) lukewarm water and mix until well combined – you may need to add a little more water if the mixture is too dry. Knead for about 10 minutes, or until the pastry is elastic. Cover with plastic wrap and set aside while preparing the filling.

To make the filling, heat the oil in a saucepan over low heat. Add the garlic, ginger and half the onion and cook until the onion has softened. Add the curry powder, salt and vinegar and mix well. Increase the heat to high, add the beef and cook, stirring constantly, until the meat changes colour. Reduce the heat to low, add 125 ml (4 fl oz/½ cup) hot water, cover, and cook until the meat is tender and all the liquid has been absorbed. Towards the end of cooking, stir frequently to prevent the meat from sticking to the base of the pan. Sprinkle with the garam masala and mint, then remove from the heat and allow to cool. Mix in the remaining chopped onion.

Take a small piece of pastry at a time, shape into a ball and roll out on a lightly floured work surface to make a circle with a 10 cm (4 in) diameter. Cut each circle in half. Put a teaspoon of filling in the centre of each half circle and brush the edges with a little water. Fold the pastry over and press the edges together firmly. You will now have a triangular-shaped samoosa. Repeat until all the pastry and filling is used.

Heat the oil in a large heavy-based saucepan over medium heat. When the oil is hot, deep-fry the samoosa, a few at a time, until golden brown. Drain on paper towel and serve hot with Fresh coriander chutney (page 168).

Singara
Savoury pastries

Makes: 32–36

2 large boiled potatoes, peeled and diced

½ teaspoon chilli powder

½ teaspoon panch phora (page 15)

1 teaspoon ground cumin

1 teaspoon salt

2 tablespoons lemon juice

1 quantity Samoosa pastry (page 47)

oil or ghee for deep-frying

To make the filling, put the potato in a bowl with the chilli powder, panch phora, cumin, salt and lemon juice and mix well to combine, being careful not to break up the potato.

Take a small piece of pastry at a time, shape into a ball and roll out on a lightly floured work surface to make a circle with a 10 cm (4 in) diameter. Cut each circle in half. Put a teaspoon of filling in the centre of each half circle and brush the edges with a little water. Fold the pastry over and press the edges together firmly. You will now have a triangular-shaped pastry. Repeat until all the pastry and filling is used.

Heat the oil in a large heavy-based saucepan over medium heat. When the oil is hot, deep-fry the singara, a few at a time, until golden brown. Drain on paper towel and serve hot.

Note

Both samoosa and singara can be made using spring roll wrappers. Cut into 6 cm (2½ in) strips the length of the pastry. Put a teaspoon of filling at one end and fold the pastry to enclose in a triangular shape. Moisten the end with a little water and press lightly to seal and enclose the filling.

Pakorhas
Savoury vegetable fritters

Makes: 24–36

Traditionally served in India at tea time, you can also serve these as an accompaniment to a meal or as a party snack. Use small pieces of raw potato, onion, cauliflower, eggplant (aubergine), zucchini (courgette) and green capsicum (bell pepper), or use a combination of your own favourites.

165 g (6 oz/1½ cups) besan (chickpea flour)

1 teaspoon garam masala (page 19)

2 teaspoons salt

½ teaspoon ground turmeric

½ teaspoon chilli powder (optional)

1 garlic clove, crushed

400 g (14 oz/4 cups) mixed chopped vegetables

oil for deep-frying

Sift the besan, garam masala, salt, turmeric and chilli powder, if using, into a bowl. Add just enough water to make a thick batter, about 250 ml (8½ fl oz/1 cup). Stir in the garlic and beat well. Set aside for 30 minutes, then beat again.

Add the vegetables to the batter and mix well.

Heat the oil in a large heavy-based saucepan over medium heat. Take one teaspoonful of the mixture at a time and gently drop into the hot oil. Cook the pakorhas in batches, turning as needed, until pale golden on both sides. Lift out with a slotted spoon and drain on paper towel. Just before serving, heat the oil again. When the oil is hot, return the pakorhas to the pan, a few at a time, for about 30 seconds, or until golden brown on both sides – the second frying makes them very crisp. Drain on paper towel and serve immediately.

Note

If you prefer to lighten the batter and lessen the strong chickpea (garbanzo bean) flavour, use half besan and half self-raising flour – a little liberty that results in puffier pakorhas, and won't topple the Taj Mahal.

Soojee Vadai
Deep-fried semolina savouries

Makes: about 10

125 g (4½ oz/1 cup) semolina	
250 ml (8½ fl oz/1 cup) boiling water	
1 small red onion, finely chopped	
1 fresh green chilli, deseeded and finely chopped	
½ teaspoon finely grated fresh ginger	
¾ teaspoon salt	
½ teaspoon ground cumin	
1 teaspoon finely chopped fresh coriander (cilantro) leaves	
oil for deep-frying	

Put the semolina in a bowl and pour over the boiling water, stirring with a wooden spoon. Add the onion, chilli, ginger, salt, cumin and coriander and mix well to make a stiff, but not dry, dough.

Take one tablespoonful of the dough at a time and press to make a flat circle with a 7.5 cm (3 in) diameter. Push a finger through the centre of the circle to make a hole in it like a doughnut.

Heat the oil in a large heavy-based saucepan over medium heat. When the oil is hot, deep-fry the savouries, in batches, turning as needed until golden all over. Drain on paper towel. Serve warm with a fresh chutney.

Thosai
South Indian pancakes

Makes: 10–12

200 g (7 oz/1 cup) long-grain rice

110 g (4 oz/½ cup) urad dal (black gram dal)

1½ teaspoons dried yeast

1 teaspoon sugar

1½ teaspoons salt

2 teaspoons ghee or oil, plus extra for
cooking

¼ teaspoon mustard seeds

1 small onion, finely chopped

1 fresh green chilli, deseeded and
finely chopped

Wash the rice and dal well, then soak each separately in a bowl of cold water for at least 8 hours or overnight. Drain well. Put the rice in a food processor with just enough water to facilitate blending. Strain through a fine sieve and set aside. Remove the skins if you are using unhusked dal, then place in a food processor or blender, adding just enough water to make a very smooth batter. Combine the ground rice and dal and mix well.

Sprinkle the yeast into a bowl with 125 ml (4 fl oz/½ cup) warm water and leave for 5 minutes to soften. Stir to dissolve, then add the sugar and salt, mixing well. Add this to the ground rice and dal, mix well and set aside in a warm place until the mixture doubles in size.

Heat the ghee in a small saucepan over low heat. Add the mustard seeds and cook them until they start to pop. Add the onion and chilli and continue cooking, stirring occasionally, until the onions are golden brown. Remove from the heat, allow to cool, then stir into the rice mixture – it should now be of a thick pouring consistency; add a little water or coconut milk if you need to thin it out a little.

Heat a little extra ghee in a pancake pan or heavy-based frying pan over low heat. Pour in just enough batter to cover the base of the pan and cook each pancake until golden brown on the bottom, then turn and cook the other side until golden. Remove to a plate and keep warm while cooking the remainder. Serve the pancakes with fresh chutneys and potato bhaji (page 148).

Thosai
Rice pancakes

Makes: about 10

265 g (9½ oz/1½ cups) rice flour

225 g (8 oz/1½ cups) plain (all-purpose) flour

2 tablespoons plain yoghurt

1 teaspoon salt, or to taste

ghee or oil for cooking

Sift the rice and plain flours into a bowl. Combine the yoghurt, salt and 625 ml (21 fl oz/2½ cups) water in a separate bowl, then add to the flour and beat with a wooden spoon to make a thick, smooth batter. Set aside in a warm place overnight, or until the mixture ferments.

Heat a little ghee in a heavy-based frying pan over low heat. Pour in just enough batter to cover the base of the pan and cook each thosai until golden brown on the bottom, then turn and cook the other side until golden. Remove to a plate and keep warm while cooking the remainder. Serve hot with dry vegetable dishes, fresh chutneys and sambals.

Pani Puri
Semolina wafers

Makes: about 80

If you met these delicious little savouries in Maharashtra State, you probably know them as pani puri; in the Punjab they are called gol gappa; and if you spent time in Calcutta you may recognise them under the name of pushka. They are typical of Indian savoury snacks for between-meal nibbling. The crisp wafers, puffed up like Lilliputian balloons, are filled to individual taste.

The snack consists of fried wafers so thin and crisp that a finger pushed through one side makes a neat little hole into which you drop two or three cooked and spiced chickpeas (garbanzo beans), a couple of cubes of potato and a teaspoonful of piquant tamarind juice. There are variations on the theme, with some versions favouring crisp fried lentils, chips of fresh coconut and fresh chutneys.

60 g (2 oz/½ cup) fine semolina

75 g (2¾ oz/½ cup) roti flour or plain (all-purpose) flour

2 teaspoons besan (chickpea flour) (optional)

½ teaspoon salt

oil for deep-frying

ghee for deep-frying

Accompaniments

Channa (savoury chickpeas) (page 44)

Channa ki dal (savoury split peas) (page 44)

Alu bhaji (savoury fried potatoes) (page 148)

Imli chatni (tamarind chutney) (page 166)

Podina chatni (mint chutney) (page 166)

Zeera pani (cumin and tamarind water) (page 194)

Put the semolina, flour, besan, if using, and salt into a bowl. Add 125 ml (4 fl oz/½ cup) lukewarm water all at once and mix to make a dough. Knead the dough for 10 minutes, adding a little more flour if the mixture is too soft, or a few drops of water if it is too stiff. (Flours vary in absorbency and it is difficult to give an exact measure of water, but the dough should be the consistency of bread dough.) Cover the dough with a small bowl or with plastic wrap and let it rest for at least 30 minutes.

Pinch off small pieces of the dough and roll each into a ball the size of a hazelnut without its shell. Roll out each ball on a lightly floured work surface to make a thin circle, with a 5 cm (2 in) diameter. Place on a tray and cover with a damp tea towel (dish towel) to prevent drying out. Allow the pastry to rest for 10–15 minutes before cooking.

Heat the oil in a large heavy-based frying pan over medium heat. When the oil is hot, deep-fry the semolina wafers, 2 or 3 at a time, spooning the hot oil over the tops of each to make them puff up. Do not add too many at a time, for this brings down the temperature of the oil and results in greasy wafers. When they are golden on both sides, remove them from the pan using a slotted spoon and drain on paper towel over a wire rack (this helps to keep them crisp when they cool). Repeat with the remaining wafers until all are cooked. If you are not serving at once, cool completely and store in an airtight container – they will keep for up to 3 days. Serve with the assorted accompaniments once cool.

Soups

*

Rasam
Pepper water

Serves: 6

These thin soups are served as an aid to digestion and are part of every meal in South India. They may be used to moisten rice, or sipped with the meal. Less frequently, they may be served as a course on their own.

1 tablespoon tamarind pulp

2 garlic cloves, sliced

¼ teaspoon asafoetida (glossary)

¾ teaspoon freshly ground black pepper

1 teaspoon ground cumin

2 teaspoons salt

2 tablespoons chopped fresh coriander (cilantro) leaves

2 teaspoons oil

1 teaspoon black mustard seeds

8 curry leaves

Soak the tamarind pulp in 250 ml (8½ fl oz/1 cup) hot water for 10 minutes. Squeeze to dissolve the pulp in the water, then strain, discarding the seeds and fibres.

Put the tamarind liquid, garlic, asafoetida, pepper, cumin, salt, coriander and 1 litre (34 fl oz/4 cups) water into a saucepan and bring to the boil. Reduce the heat to low and simmer for 10 minutes.

Heat the oil in a separate frying pan and cook the mustard seeds and curry leaves until the leaves are brown. Add to the simmering liquid, divide among bowls and serve immediately.

Dal Rasam
Pepper water with lentils

Serves: 6

125 g (4½ oz/½ cup) red lentils

1 small cinnamon stick

3 whole cloves

10 whole black peppercorns

2 small onions

2 teaspoons salt

2 teaspoons ghee or oil

lemon juice to taste

250 ml (8½ fl oz/1 cup) coconut milk (optional) (pages 6–8)

Rinse the lentils, drain well, then place in a saucepan with the cinnamon stick, cloves, peppercorns, 1 of the onions, the salt and 1 litre (34 fl oz/4 cups) water. Bring to the boil, then reduce the heat to low and simmer until the lentils are very soft. Push the lentils and onion through a sieve, discarding the whole spices. Set aside.

Thinly slice the remaining onion. Heat the ghee in a frying pan over low heat and cook the onion until quite brown. Add the lentil liquid and lemon juice and season with extra salt, to taste. If a richer rasam is preferred, add the coconut milk at the end of cooking and adjust the seasoning, to taste. Divide among serving bowls and serve hot.

Soups ✦

Yakhni
Basic stock

Serves: 6

Many recipes require a rich, spicy stock for cooking rice for pilaus and birianis. This versatile stock recipe can be made using lamb, chicken or beef. For economy, the lamb stock is made with bones taken from the leg or loin, plus two or three lamb shanks. Chicken frames, backs and necks are often sold separately, are much cheaper than other joints, and are ideal for stock, as bones add the most flavour.

500 g (1 lb 2 oz) chicken, lamb or beef

6 whole cardamom pods, bruised

1 large onion

6 whole cloves

1 teaspoon whole black peppercorns

Put all the ingredients into a stockpot or large saucepan with 2–2.5 litres (68–85 fl oz/8–10 cups) water and bring to the boil. Reduce the heat to low and simmer, skimming the surface during the first few minutes to remove any impurities. Cover and simmer for 1½–2 hours.

Remove from the heat and cool, then refrigerate for about 3 hours to chill. Remove any fat from the surface before using. Store in an airtight container in the refrigerator for up to 1 week or freeze for up to 3 months.

Sambar
Lentil and vegetable soup

Serves: 6

220 g (8 oz/1 cup) yellow split peas or
   red lentils

1 tablespoon tamarind pulp

2 tablespoons ghee or oil

1 tablespoon ground coriander

2 teaspoons ground cumin

½ teaspoon freshly ground black pepper

½ teaspoon ground turmeric

¼ teaspoon asafoetida (glossary)

2 fresh green chillies, deseeded and sliced

2½ teaspoons salt

500 g (1 lb 2 oz/5 cups) mixed chopped
   vegetables, such as eggplant (aubergine),
   carrot, marrow (summer squash)
   and beans

½ teaspoon black mustard seeds or
   panch phora (page 15)

1 small onion, thinly sliced

Rinse the split peas, drain well then leave to soak in a bowl of fresh water for at least 2 hours, or overnight. Drain well.

Put the split peas in a large saucepan with 1.5 litres (51 fl oz/6 cups) water and bring to the boil, then reduce the heat to low and simmer until softened.

Meanwhile, soak the tamarind pulp in 250 ml (8½ fl oz/ 1 cup) hot water for 10 minutes. Squeeze to dissolve the pulp in the water, then strain, discarding the seeds and fibres. Add the tamarind liquid to the lentils.

Heat 1 tablespoon of the oil in a saucepan over low heat. Add the coriander, cumin, pepper, turmeric and asafoetida and stir for 1–2 minutes, then add to the lentils along with the chilli, salt and vegetables. Cook for about 30 minutes, or until the vegetables are soft.

Heat the remaining oil in a separate pan and fry the mustard seeds and onion until the onion has browned. Add to the lentil mixture and continue simmering for a further 1–2 minutes, stirring well to combine. Remove from the heat, divide among serving bowls and serve immediately.

Note

If tamarind pulp is unavailable, use lemon juice to taste, adding at the end of cooking.

Mulligatawny

Serves: 8–10

This curry-flavoured soup derives its name from the Tamil *mulegoothani,* or pepper water. Mulligatawny as we know it is the Anglo-Indian version, made with beef, chicken or fish stock. This recipe includes coconut milk, which gives it a wonderful richness and delicious flavour.

Beef Stock

1 kg (2 lb 3 oz) beef shank (shin)

1 kg (2 lb 3 oz) soup (beef) bones

6 cardamom pods

1 tablespoon curry leaves

2 tablespoons coriander seeds

1 tablespoon cumin seeds

1 garlic clove

12 whole black peppercorns

2 teaspoons salt

1 tablespoon tamarind pulp or
   2 tablespoons lemon juice

1 onion

3 whole cloves

20 g (¾ oz) ghee

2 onions, thinly sliced

½ teaspoon black mustard seeds

8 curry leaves

750 ml (25½ fl oz/3 cups) coconut milk
   (pages 6–8)

salt to taste

To make the stock, put the beef and bones in a stockpot or large saucepan with enough water to cover. Add the cardamom pods, curry leaves, coriander and cumin seeds, garlic, peppercorns, salt, tamarind pulp and whole onion studded with the cloves. Bring to the boil, then reduce the heat to low and simmer for 1–2 hours, or until the beef is tender and the stock is reduced by half. Remove from the heat and allow to cool slightly. Remove the beef and bones, discarding the bones. Strain the stock – you should have about 1.5 litres (51 fl oz/6 cups) of stock. Cut the beef into small cubes and reserve.

Heat the ghee in a large saucepan over medium heat. Add the onion and cook until dark brown. Add the mustard seeds and curry leaves and stir for 1–2 minutes, then add the warm stock – it will hiss and spit, so be careful. Simmer for 5 minutes, then add the coconut milk, stir to combine and remove from the heat. Season with salt, to taste. Add the lemon juice now if you are not using the tamarind pulp. Return the diced beef to the soup, stir to combine, and serve hot.

Seafood

✴

Machchi Molee
Fish cooked in coconut milk

Serves: 4

500 g (1 lb 2 oz) skinless, boneless, firm
  white fish fillets or steaks

½ teaspoon ground turmeric

1 teaspoon salt

1 tablespoon ghee or oil

1 onion, thinly sliced

2 garlic cloves, finely chopped

1 teaspoon finely grated fresh ginger

8 curry leaves

2–3 fresh red or green chillies, halved
  lengthways and deseeded

500 ml (17 fl oz/2 cups) thin coconut milk
  (pages 6–8)

250 ml (8½ fl oz/1 cup) thick coconut milk
  (pages 6–8)

lime or lemon juice to taste

Wash the fish and pat dry with paper towel. Rub over the combined turmeric and salt and set aside.

Heat the ghee in a saucepan over medium heat. Add the onion, garlic, ginger, curry leaves and chilli and cook, stirring constantly, until the onion has softened, being careful that it doesn't brown. Add the thin coconut milk and stir while it comes to simmering point. Add the fish and simmer, uncovered, for 10 minutes. Add the thick coconut milk and stir to heat through. Remove the pan from the heat before adding the lime juice and salt to taste. Serve with rice.

Machchi Tamatar Ki Kari
Fish curry with tomato

Serves: 4

500 g (1 lb 2 oz) fish fillets or steaks

2 tablespoons ghee or oil

1 onion, finely chopped

2 garlic cloves, finely chopped

2 tablespoons chopped fresh coriander (cilantro) or mint leaves

1 teaspoon ground cumin

1 teaspoon ground turmeric

½–1 teaspoon chilli powder, or to taste

1 large ripe tomato, chopped

1 teaspoon salt

1½ teaspoons garam masala (page 19)

lemon juice to taste

Wash the fish and pat dry with paper towel, then cut each fillet into serving pieces (see page 11).

Heat the ghee in a saucepan over low heat. Add the onion, garlic and coriander, and cook, stirring regularly, until the onion has softened. Add the cumin, turmeric and chilli powder and stir until the spices are cooked and aromatic.

Add the tomato, salt and garam masala to the pan and continue cooking until the tomato is cooked to a pulp. Add the lemon juice, to taste, and check if more salt is needed. Put the pieces of fish into the tomato, spooning it over the fish, then cover the pan and simmer for 10 minutes, or until the fish is cooked through. Serve immediately with rice.

Machchi Kari
Fish curry

Serves: 4

Strong curries are particularly suited to strong flavoured fish with dark flesh, such as kingfish, tuna, trevally or small fish, such as sardines or anchovies. Fenugreek is almost always used in these types of curries.

500 g (1 lb 2 oz) skinless, boneless fish fillets, such as kingfish, tuna or trevally, or small whole fish, such as sardines or anchovies

2 tablespoons oil

6–8 curry leaves

1 onion, thinly sliced

2 garlic cloves, thinly sliced

1 tablespoon finely grated fresh ginger

1 tablespoon ground coriander

2 teaspoons ground cumin

½ teaspoon ground turmeric

½–1 teaspoon chilli powder

½ teaspoon ground fenugreek

500 ml (17 fl oz/2 cups) coconut milk (pages 6–8)

1½ teaspoons salt, or to taste

lemon juice to taste

Wash the fish and pat dry with paper towel. Cut the large fish fillets into serving pieces (see page 11). If small fish are used, clean and scale them.

Heat the oil in a large frying pan over low heat. Add the curry leaves and cook until slightly brown, then add the onion, garlic and ginger and cook, stirring constantly, until the onion has softened. Add all the ground spices and cook, stirring regularly, until they become aromatic. Add the coconut milk and salt and bring to the boil, then reduce the heat to low and simmer, uncovered, for 10 minutes.

Add the fish to the pan, spooning the liquid over the fish, and continue simmering until the fish is cooked through. Remove from the heat and stir in the lemon juice, to taste. Serve immediately with rice.

Khattai Wali Machchi Kari
Sour fish curry

Serves: 4

500 g (1 lb 2 oz) skinless, boneless fish
   fillets, such as kingfish, tuna or trevally,
   or small whole fish, such as sardines or
   anchovies

1 tablespoon tamarind pulp

1 onion, chopped

3 garlic cloves

1 teaspoon finely chopped fresh ginger

1 tablespoon ground coriander

2 teaspoons ground cumin

1 teaspoon ground turmeric

1 teaspoon chilli powder

½ teaspoon ground fenugreek

60 ml (2 fl oz/¼ cup) vegetable oil

1 tablespoon vinegar or lemon juice

1½ teaspoons salt

Wash the fish and pat dry with paper towel. Cut the large fish fillets into serving pieces (see page 11). If small fish are used, clean and scale them.

Soak the tamarind pulp in 125 ml (4 fl oz/½ cup) hot water for 10 minutes. Squeeze to dissolve the pulp in the water, then strain, discarding the seeds and fibres.

Put the onion, garlic, ginger and 1 tablespoon of the tamarind liquid in a food processor and process to make a smooth purée. Mix in the ground spices.

Heat the oil in a saucepan over medium heat. Add the onion mixture and stir until it thickens and darkens. Add the remaining tamarind liquid, vinegar and salt, then pour in just enough hot water to cover the fish. Bring to the boil, then add the fish and simmer until cooked through.

Note

If you cannot obtain tamarind pulp, use tamarind purée that comes in jars, but add 1½ tablespoons, as it is not generally as acid as the pulp. As always, be guided by taste.

Masala Dum Machchi
Spiced baked fish

Serves: 4

1 kg (2 lb 3 oz) whole fish, cleaned, scaled, head removed

salt

lemon juice

oil

1 tablespoon finely chopped fresh ginger

3 garlic cloves, finely chopped

1 fresh red chilli, deseeded and chopped, plus extra to garnish

1 teaspoon ground cumin

1 teaspoon garam masala (page 19)

250 g (9 oz/1 cup) plain yoghurt

fresh coriander (cilantro) leaves to garnish

Wipe out the cavity of the fish with paper towel dipped in coarse salt, then wash well. Rub the cavity with a little salt and lemon juice. Pat the outside dry with paper towel. Make diagonal slits in the flesh on each side of the fish and place in a large baking tray.

Heat the oil in a large heavy-based frying pan over medium heat. Add the ginger, garlic and chilli and cook until softened. Add the cumin and garam masala and cook for 2–3 minutes, then remove from the heat and stir into the yoghurt until well combined. Season with salt to taste.

Preheat the oven to 180°C (350°F). Spread the marinade on both sides of the fish, making sure it goes into the cuts and inside the cavity. Leave to stand at room temperature for 30 minutes, then bake in the oven for 35 minutes, or until the flesh is white and opaque. Garnish with the coriander leaves and chilli, and serve hot.

Tali Machchi (1)
Fried fish (1)

Serves: 4

Use tuna, jewfish, Spanish mackerel, kingfish or any firm fish.

750 g (1 lb 11 oz) fish fillets or steaks

2 garlic cloves

1½ teaspoons salt

1 teaspoon finely grated fresh ginger

½ teaspoon ground turmeric

½ teaspoon ground black pepper

¼ teaspoon chilli powder (optional)

lemon juice

oil for frying

fresh coriander (cilantro) leaves to garnish

lemon wedges to garnish

Wash the fish and pat dry with paper towel.

Pound the garlic and salt using a mortar and pestle. Then mix in a bowl with the ginger, turmeric, pepper, chilli powder, if using, and enough lemon juice to make a paste. Rub the paste over the fish on both sides, cover, and leave to marinate for 20 minutes.

Heat the oil in a large heavy-based frying pan over medium heat and cook the fish on both sides.

Remove from the heat and serve the fish on a serving platter garnished with the coriander leaves and lemon wedges.

Tali Machchi (2)
Fried fish (2)

Serves: 4

500 g (1 lb 2 oz) skinless, boneless firm white fish fillets

3 tablespoons besan (chickpea flour)

3 tablespoons plain (all-purpose) flour

1½ teaspoons salt

1 teaspoon garam masala (page 19)

½ teaspoon ground turmeric

oil for deep-frying

1 egg, well beaten

Wash the fish and pat dry with paper towel.

Mix together the besan, plain flour, salt, garam masala and turmeric in a bowl.

Heat the oil in a large heavy-based saucepan over medium heat. Gently lower the fish fillets first into the egg, then turn to coat with the flour mixture, shaking off any excess. When the oil is hot, deep-fry the fish until golden brown. Drain on paper towel and serve immediately with rice, pickles and Eggplant purée (page 151).

Jhinga Bhajia
Prawn fritters

Makes: about 20

250 g (9 oz) raw prawns (shrimp), peeled, deveined and finely chopped

1 small onion, finely chopped

1 garlic clove, crushed

½ teaspoon salt

1 teaspoon finely grated fresh ginger

1 tablespoon finely chopped fresh coriander (cilantro) leaves

¼ teaspoon freshly ground black pepper

½ teaspoon ground cumin

½ teaspoon garam masala (page 19)

2 tablespoons besan (chickpea flour)

2 tablespoons plain (all-purpose) flour

oil for deep-frying

Combine the prawns in a bowl with the onion, garlic, salt, ginger, coriander, pepper, cumin and garam masala.

In a separate bowl, mix together the besan and plain flour.

Take 1 tablespoon of the prawn mixture at a time and use your hands to roll into small balls. Roll in the flour to coat, shaking off any excess.

Heat the oil in a large heavy-based saucepan over medium heat. When the oil is hot, deep-fry the prawn balls, in batches, spooning the oil over as they cook, until they are golden brown all over. Drain on paper towel and serve hot.

Machchi Kebab
Grilled fish on skewers

Serves: 6

Use fish of a good thickness, such as snapper (porgy), hake or jewfish, for it is difficult to thread very thin slices of fish onto skewers.

1 kg (2 lb 3 oz) boneless firm white fish fillets, skin on

2 teaspoons finely grated fresh ginger

3 garlic cloves, crushed

1½ teaspoons salt

1 tablespoon ground coriander

1 teaspoon garam masala (page 19)

½ teaspoon chilli powder

1 teaspoon amchur powder or 3 tablespoons lemon juice

250 g (9 oz/1 cup) plain yoghurt

2 tablespoons plain (all-purpose) flour

Wash the fish and pat dry with paper towel. Cut the fish into 4 cm (1½ in) pieces. Soak 12 bamboo skewers in water to prevent them from burning during cooking.

Mix together the remaining ingredients in a bowl to make a marinade. Pour over the fish pieces and gently toss to coat. Leave for 15 minutes at room temperature, or longer in the refrigerator.

Preheat the grill (broiler) and while it is heating, thread 4 or 5 pieces of fish onto each bamboo skewer, making sure all the skin is on one side of the skewer.

Grill the skewers 10 cm (4 in) away from the heat with the skin side upwards, for 4 minutes. Turn the skewers and grill the other side for 4–5 minutes, depending on the thickness of the fish. Serve the fish kebabs immediately, accompanied by rice or Chapatis (page 23) and Onion sambal (page 159).

Patrani Machchi
Fish steamed in banana leaves

Serves: 4

750 g (1 lb 11 oz) skinless, boneless, firm white fish fillets or 4 × 250 g (9 oz) whole fish, scaled and cleaned

salt

banana leaves or foil for wrapping

Masala

1 large lemon

2 onions, finely chopped

1 teaspoon finely chopped fresh ginger

2 garlic cloves

2 fresh green chillies, deseeded and chopped

25 g (1 oz/½ cup) fresh coriander (cilantro) leaves, chopped

1 teaspoon ground cumin

½ teaspoon ground fenugreek

45 g (1½ oz/½ cup) freshly grated or desiccated (shredded) coconut

2 tablespoons ghee or oil

2 teaspoons salt

1 teaspoon garam masala (page 19)

Wash the fish and pat dry with paper towel. Rub over some salt and set aside while preparing the masala.

To make the masala, peel the lemon, removing all the white pith. Cut the lemon into pieces, discarding the seeds. Put the lemon into a food processor with half of the onion, the ginger, garlic, chilli, fresh coriander, cumin and fenugreek. Process until puréed, then add the coconut and process to combine.

Heat the oil in a frying pan over medium heat. Add the remaining onion and cook until golden. Add the lemon purée and cook for a few minutes, stirring to combine. Remove from the heat and add the salt and garam masala.

Coat each fish fillet with the masala mixture, wrap securely in banana leaves or foil and steam over a saucepan of gently simmering water for 30 minutes, turning parcels once halfway through cooking. Serve in the leaf parcels. Have a bowl or plate to collect the leaves as each person unwraps the fish.

Seafood ✦

Tisrya Dum Masala
Spicy steamed mussels

Serves: 4

3 tablespoons ghee or oil

2 large onions, finely chopped

4 garlic cloves, finely chopped

3 teaspoons finely chopped fresh ginger

3 fresh red chillies, deseeded and chopped

½ teaspoon ground turmeric

3 teaspoons ground coriander

a pinch of chilli powder (optional)

½ teaspoon salt

1 kg (2 lb 3 oz) fresh mussels, scrubbed and beards removed

1 tablespoon chopped fresh coriander (cilantro) leaves

lemon juice to taste

Heat the ghee in a large heavy-based saucepan over medium heat. Add the onion, garlic and ginger and cook until the onion is golden. Add the chilli, turmeric, ground coriander and chilli powder, if using, and stir for 3 minutes, then add the salt and 250 ml (8½ fl oz/1 cup) water and bring to the boil. Reduce the heat and simmer, covered, for 5 minutes.

Add the mussels to the pan, cover, and continue to simmer for 10–15 minutes, or until the shells have opened. Remove from the heat, sprinkle in the chopped coriander and season with salt and lemon juice, to taste, Divide the mussels among serving bowls and spoon the cooking liquid over the top. Serve hot with rice.

Note

Do not use any mussels that are not tightly closed before cooking, and discard any that do not open during cooking.

Jhinga Kari
South Indian prawn curry

Serves: 4–6

If cooked prawns (shrimp) are used in this recipe, add them during the last 10 minutes. The paprika is used to give the curry the desired red colour, which in India would come from the large number of chillies or chilli powder used.

1 tablespoon desiccated (shredded) coconut

1 tablespoon ground rice

500 ml (17 fl oz/2 cups) coconut milk
  (pages 6–8)

2 tablespoons ghee or oil

12 curry leaves

2 onions, finely chopped

5 garlic cloves, finely chopped

3 teaspoons finely grated fresh ginger

2 tablespoons Madras-style curry paste
  (page 20)

1 teaspoon chilli powder (optional)

2 teaspoons paprika

1½ teaspoons salt

1 kg (2 lb 3 oz) raw prawns (shrimp), peeled
  and deveined

2 tablespoons lemon juice

Put the desiccated coconut into a dry frying pan and toast over medium heat, shaking the pan or stirring constantly until the coconut is golden brown. Remove to a plate and repeat with the ground rice. Put the toasted coconut and ground rice into a food processor with 125 ml (4 fl oz/½ cup) of the coconut milk and process until smooth.

Heat the ghee in a saucepan over low heat. Add the curry leaves and cook for 1 minute. Add the onion, garlic and ginger and cook until golden brown, stirring with a wooden spoon. Add the curry powder, chilli powder, if using, and paprika and cook over low heat, stirring well – do not let the spices burn. Add the coconut mixture, the remaining coconut milk and salt, stirring until it starts to simmer – do not cover. Simmer gently for about 15 minutes, stirring occasionally.

Add the prawns to the pan, stir to combine, and simmer for a further 10–15 minutes, or until the prawns are cooked and the sauce has thickened. Stir in the lemon juice and serve hot with rice.

Jhinga Molee
Prawns in coconut milk

Serves: 4

A *molee* is a South Indian preparation in which the main ingredient is cooked in rich coconut milk; it is also used in Sri Lanka and among Malays and is often called a 'white curry'. It is deliciously mild. Coconut milk being the main ingredient, the pan must not be covered at any time during cooking and the liquid should be stirred while coming to the boil to prevent curdling.

750 g (1 lb 11 oz) raw large prawns (shrimp)

2 tablespoons ghee or oil

2 onions, thinly sliced

2 garlic cloves, crushed

1 teaspoon finely grated fresh ginger

2 fresh red or green chillies, halved lengthways and deseeded

1 teaspoon ground turmeric

8 curry leaves

500 ml (17 fl oz/2 cups) coconut milk (pages 6–8)

1 teaspoon salt

lemon juice to taste

Shell and devein the prawns if you like, but some local cooks say the prawns should be in their shells, for they retain more flavour this way. If you leave the heads on it is still possible to devein the prawns by inserting the tip of a sharp knife or a thin skewer behind the head and teasing out the intestinal tract.

Heat the ghee in a large heavy-based frying pan over medium heat. Add the onion, garlic and ginger and cook until the onion has softened but not browned. Add the chilli, turmeric and curry leaves and cook for 1 minute, then add the coconut milk and salt and stir until it starts to simmer. Simmer, uncovered, for 10 minutes, then add the prawns and cook for 10–15 minutes, or until opaque.

Remove from the heat and add the lemon juice, to taste. Serve hot.

Eggs

*

Anda Kari
Egg curry

Serves: 4–6

2 tablespoons ghee or oil

2 onions, finely chopped

3 garlic cloves, finely chopped

2 teaspoons finely grated fresh ginger

3 teaspoons ground coriander

2 teaspoons ground cumin

1 teaspoon ground turmeric

½ teaspoon chilli powder

2–3 ripe tomatoes, diced

1 teaspoon salt, or to taste

½ teaspoon garam masala (page 19)

6 large hard-boiled eggs, peeled and halved

Heat the ghee in a large heavy-based frying pan over low heat. Add the onion, garlic and ginger and cook until the onion has softened and is golden brown. Add the coriander, cumin, turmeric and chilli powder and cook for a few seconds, then add the tomato and salt and stir over medium heat until the tomatoes are soft and pulpy. Add 125 ml (4 fl oz/½ cup) hot water, cover, and simmer until the sauce is thick, then stir in the garam masala and the eggs and heat through. Serve hot with rice.

Eggs

Akoori

Parsi scrambled eggs

Serves: 4–6

....

6–8 large eggs, lightly beaten

80 ml (2½ fl oz/⅓ cup) milk

¾ teaspoon salt

¼ teaspoon freshly ground black pepper

40 g (1½ oz) ghee

6 spring onions (scallions), finely chopped

2–3 fresh red or green chillies, deseeded
and chopped

1 teaspoon finely grated fresh ginger

⅛ teaspoon ground turmeric

2 tablespoons chopped fresh coriander
(cilantro) leaves, plus extra to garnish

1 ripe tomato, diced (optional), plus extra
to garnish

½ teaspoon ground cumin

Combine the eggs and milk in a bowl with the salt
and pepper.

Heat the ghee in a large heavy-based frying pan over low
heat. Add the spring onion, chilli and ginger and cook until
the onion has softened. Add the turmeric, coriander and
tomato, if using, and cook for 1–2 minutes further, then stir
in the egg mixture and the ground cumin. Cook over low
heat, stirring and lifting the eggs as they begin to set on the
base of the pan. Mix and cook until the eggs are of a creamy
consistency – they should not be cooked until dry.

Remove the eggs to a serving plate and garnish with the
tomato and coriander. Serve with Chapatis (page 23) or
Paratha (page 28).

Mootay Molee
Eggs in coconut milk gravy

Serves: 4–6

Among the South Indian Tamils, this is a favourite way of serving eggs.

2 tablespoons ghee or oil

1 large onion, thinly sliced

3 garlic cloves, finely chopped

2 teaspoons finely grated fresh ginger

3 fresh green chillies, deseeded and
thinly sliced

6 curry leaves

1 teaspoon ground turmeric

500 ml (17 fl oz/2 cups) thin coconut milk
(pages 6–8)

375 ml (12½ fl oz/1½ cups) thick coconut
milk (pages 6–8)

1 teaspoon salt, or to taste

6 large hard-boiled eggs, peeled and halved

2 tablespoons lemon juice, or to taste

Heat the ghee in a frying pan over low heat. Add the onion, garlic, ginger, chilli and curry leaves and cook until the onion has softened – do not let it colour. Add the turmeric and stir for 1 minute, then add the thin coconut milk and simmer gently, uncovered, for 10 minutes. Add the thick coconut milk and salt and stir constantly as it comes to simmering point, then add the eggs and simmer, uncovered, for a further 6–7 minutes. Remove from the heat, stir in the lemon juice, to taste, and serve hot with rice.

Poultry

✤

Murgh Biriani
Muslim-style chicken biriani

Serves: 6

For biriani, always use long-grain rice. Basmati rice with its thin, fine grains is the ideal variety to use in this festive dish.

Chicken savoury

1.25 kg (2 lb 12 oz) chicken or chicken pieces

100 g (3½ oz) ghee or 100 ml (3½ fl oz) oil

2 tablespoons blanched almonds

2 tablespoons sultanas (golden raisins)

4 small potatoes, peeled and halved

2 large onions, finely chopped

5 garlic cloves, finely chopped

1 tablespoon finely chopped fresh ginger

½ teaspoon chilli powder

½ teaspoon freshly ground black pepper

½ teaspoon ground turmeric

1 teaspoon ground cumin

1 teaspoon salt

2 tomatoes, peeled and chopped

2 tablespoons plain yoghurt

2 tablespoons chopped mint leaves

½ teaspoon ground cardamom

5 cm (2 in) piece cinnamon stick

Biriani rice

500 g (1 lb 2 oz/2½ cups) basmati rice

2½ tablespoons ghee

1 large onion, finely chopped

⅛ teaspoon saffron strands

5 cardamom pods

3 whole cloves

1 cinnamon stick

½ teaspoon kencur (aromatic ginger) powder (glossary)

2 tablespoons rosewater

1½ teaspoons salt

1 litre (34 fl oz/4 cups) strong chicken stock (page 58)

Note

If liked, more colour can be added to this dish by garnishing with quartered hard-boiled eggs and cooked green peas.

To make the chicken savoury, joint the chicken (see page 10) and cut into serving pieces.

Heat half of the ghee in a small frying pan and cook the almonds until golden, then remove to a plate. Add the sultanas to the pan and cook for a few seconds, then remove to a plate and set aside. Cook the potato halves until brown, then remove to a plate.

Pour any ghee left in the pan into a large saucepan; add the remaining ghee and cook the onion, garlic and ginger until golden. Add the chilli powder, pepper, turmeric, cumin, salt and tomato and stir constantly for 5 minutes. Add the yoghurt, mint, cardamom and cinnamon stick, cover, and cook over low heat, stirring occasionally, until the tomato has cooked to a pulp. (It may be necessary to add a little hot water if the mixture becomes too dry and starts to stick to the pan.) When the mixture is thick and smooth, add the chicken pieces and stir well to coat. Cover and continue cooking over low heat until the chicken is tender, about 35–45 minutes – there should only be a little very thick gravy left when the chicken is cooked; if necessary cook uncovered for a few minutes to reduce the gravy.

To make the biriani rice, wash the rice well and drain in a colander for 30 minutes. Heat the ghee in a large heavy-based saucepan over medium heat. Add the onion and cook until golden. Add the saffron strands, cardamom pods, cloves, cinnamon stick, kencur powder and rice and stir to coat the rice. Add the rosewater and salt to the hot stock, then pour over the rice in the pan and stir well. Add the chicken savoury and potatoes and gently mix into the rice. Bring to the boil, then reduce the heat to low, cover, and steam for 20 minutes, or until the rice is tender – do not lift the lid or stir while cooking.

To serve, spoon the biriani into a serving dish and garnish with the almonds and sultanas. Serve immediately with Onion sambal (page 159), Cucumber with yoghurt (page 159) and hot pickles.

Murgh Musallam
Whole chicken in spices and yoghurt

Serves: 6

....

1.5 kg (3 lb 5 oz) whole chicken

¼ teaspoon saffron strands

½ teaspoon freshly ground black pepper

½ teaspoon ground turmeric

½ teaspoon ground cumin

½ teaspoon chilli powder

¼ teaspoon ground cardamom

¼ teaspoon ground cloves

¼ teaspoon ground cinnamon

¼ teaspoon ground mace

2 garlic cloves, crushed

1½ teaspoons salt

2 tablespoons plain yoghurt

3 tablespoons ghee or oil

2 onions, thinly sliced

310 ml (10½ fl oz/1¼ cups) hot water or stock

Wipe the chicken inside and out with damp paper towel, removing the neck and giblets and cutting off the wing tips.

Gently heat the saffron strands in a frying pan over low heat for 1–2 minutes, shaking the pan frequently and making sure they don't burn. Remove to a plate to cool and crisp, then crush to a powder in a cup, adding 1 tablespoon of hot water to dissolve. Mix together all the ground spices and the garlic crushed with salt, into the yoghurt and stir into the dissolved saffron. Rub a tablespoon of the mixture inside the cavity of the chicken, then rub another tablespoonful over the outside. Leave to marinate for 1 hour.

Heat the ghee in a large heavy-based saucepan over medium heat. Add the onion and cook until golden. Remove to a plate, then add the chicken to the pan and brown lightly on all sides. Return the onions to the pan. Stir the remaining marinade into the hot water and add to the pan. Bring to the boil, then reduce the heat to low, cover, and simmer for 45 minutes, or until the chicken is very tender. (Turn the chicken from time to time so it cooks first on one side and then the other.) The liquid should evaporate almost completely. Serve hot.

Murgh Kaleja Kari
Chicken liver curry

Serves: 4

500 g (1 lb 2 oz) chicken livers

2 tablespoons ghee or oil

1 large onion, finely chopped

2 garlic cloves, finely chopped

2 tablespoons finely grated fresh ginger

½ teaspoon ground turmeric

1 teaspoon chilli powder

3 teaspoons ground coriander

2 teaspoons ground cumin

1 teaspoon garam masala (page 19)

1 ripe tomato, chopped

1 teaspoon salt

½ teaspoon freshly ground black pepper

Wash and drain the chicken livers. Cut each one in half, and discard any yellow spots.

Heat the ghee in a frying pan over low heat. Add the onion, garlic and ginger and cook until the onion is golden brown. Add the turmeric, chilli powder, coriander and cumin and cook for 2 minutes, stirring often. Add the garam masala, tomato and salt and cook, covered, until the tomato is pulpy. Stir and mash the tomato with a wooden spoon to speed up the process. Add the chicken livers, stir well, sprinkle over the pepper, cover, and cook for 15–20 minutes, or until the livers are firm and pale pink. Serve hot with rice.

Masala Murgh
Grilled masala chicken

Serves: 4–6

An easy way to cook spiced chicken, using some of the excellent masala mixtures available in paste and powder form.

1.25 kg (2 lb 12 oz) whole chicken or
  6 large chicken drumsticks

1 teaspoon tandoori mix (page 16)

1 teaspoon Green masala paste (page 21)

1 teaspoon salt

3 teaspoons sesame oil

3 teaspoons ground rice

½ teaspoon garam masala (page 19)

Joint the chicken (see page 10) and cut into serving pieces. Use a sharp knife to score the skin and flesh halfway to the bone.

Combine all the remaining ingredients in a bowl with 1½ tablespoons water and rub all over the chicken, pressing some into the cuts. Set aside for at least 30 minutes to marinate (or you can cover the chicken and refrigerate it overnight).

Preheat the grill (broiler) to high and put the chicken on the rack, skin side down. Position the rack at the furthest point from the heat and grill for 10–15 minutes. Turn the chicken pieces over and grill for a further 10 minutes, or until the juices run clear when pierced with a knife. Serve hot, accompanied by rice or any of the Indian breads, and a sambal or raita.

Kaju Murgh Kari
Curried chicken with cashew nuts

Serves: 6

This curry has a rich, thick sauce that makes it ideal for eating with the flatbreads of India.

1.7 kg (3 lb 12 oz) whole chicken

3 tablespoons ghee or oil

2 large onions, finely chopped

3 garlic cloves, finely chopped

1½ teaspoons finely grated fresh ginger

3 tablespoons Indian curry powder

1 teaspoon chilli powder (optional)

3 teaspoons salt

3 ripe tomatoes, peeled and chopped

2 tablespoons chopped fresh coriander
(cilantro) or mint leaves, plus extra
to garnish

2 teaspoons garam masala (page 19)

125 g (4½ oz/½ cup) plain yoghurt

125 g (4½ oz) raw cashew nuts,
finely ground

Joint the chicken (see page 10) and cut into serving pieces – separate the drumsticks from the thighs, wings from the breasts, and cut the breasts into four. If large, the thighs and drumsticks can be chopped in halves using a heavy cleaver and cutting through the bone. The smaller the pieces of chicken, the better the spices can penetrate.

Heat the ghee in a large saucepan over medium–low heat. Add the onion, garlic and ginger and cook until soft and golden, stirring occasionally. Add the curry powder and chilli powder, if using, and stir for 1 minute, then add the salt, tomato and coriander and cook to a pulp, stirring with a wooden spoon. Add the chicken and stir well to coat. Reduce the heat to low, cover, and simmer for 45 minutes, or until the chicken is tender, stirring with the wooden spoon every 15 minutes and scraping the base of the pan to remove any stuck-on bits. Stir in the garam masala and yoghurt and simmer, uncovered, for 5 minutes. Finally, add the cashew nuts and heat through. Scatter over the extra coriander and serve hot with Chapatis (page 23), Paratha (page 28), Puris (page 26) or rice.

Note

For a milder flavour, use paprika instead of chilli powder. It will give a good red colour without adding heat. The cashew nuts can be ground in a food processor or very finely chopped.

Kesar Murgh
Saffron chicken

Serves: 4–6

....

1.5 kg (3 lb 5 oz) whole chicken

60 g (2 oz) ghee

1 large onion, finely chopped

3 garlic cloves, finely chopped

1½ teaspoons finely grated fresh ginger

3 fresh red chillies, deseeded and sliced

¼ teaspoon saffron strands

½ teaspoon ground cardamom

1½ teaspoons salt

Joint the chicken (see page 10) and cut into serving pieces.

Heat the ghee in a heavy-based saucepan over medium heat. Add the onion, garlic, ginger and chilli and cook, stirring often, until the onion starts to turn golden.

Gently heat the saffron strands in a frying pan over low heat for 1–2 minutes, shaking the pan frequently and making sure they don't burn. Remove to a plate to cool and crisp, then crush to a powder in a cup, adding 1 tablespoon hot water to dissolve. Add the saffron mixture to the pan with the cardamom and stir well. Add the chicken, increase the heat and cook for 4–5 minutes, turning often, until each piece of chicken is golden and coated with the saffron mixture. Add the salt, cover, and cook over medium heat for 10 minutes, or until the chicken is tender. Uncover the pan and continue cooking until most of the liquid evaporates. Serve hot with Paratha (page 28) or rice.

Bhuna Murgh
Chicken dry curry

Serves: 4–5

....

1.5 kg (3 lb 5 oz) whole chicken

3 tablespoons oil or ghee

10 curry leaves, finely crumbled

½ teaspoon black mustard seeds

1 large onion, finely chopped

2–3 garlic cloves, finely chopped

1 tablespoon finely chopped fresh ginger

2 teaspoons curry powder

1 teaspoon tandoori mix (page 16)

1 teaspoon ground cumin

½ teaspoon garam masala (page 19)

1 teaspoon chilli powder or paprika

½ teaspoon amchur powder or 1 tablespoon
  lemon juice

2 teaspoons salt

Joint the chicken (see page 10) and cut into serving pieces.

Heat the oil in a large frying pan over low heat. Add the curry leaves and the mustard seeds and cook for 1 minute, then add the onion, garlic and ginger and cook until the onion is golden brown, stirring from time to time. Add the curry powder, tandoori mix, cumin, garam masala, chilli powder and amchur powder. Cook for a further 1 minute, stirring well to combine, then add the salt and lemon juice, if using. Add the chicken and turn to coat in the spice mixture. Cover the pan and cook over low heat until the chicken is tender. Stir occasionally and, if necessary, add some extra hot water, about 60–125 ml (2–4 fl oz/¼–½ cup) hot water. Serve hot with Chapatis (page 23), Paratha (page 28) or rice.

Dahi Murgh
Chicken and yoghurt curry

Serves: 4

1.5 kg (3 lb 5 oz) whole chicken

1 onion, roughly chopped

3 garlic cloves, peeled

1 teaspoon finely chopped fresh ginger

15 g (½ oz/½ cup) fresh coriander (cilantro) or mint leaves, plus extra to garnish

1½ tablespoons ghee or oil

1 teaspoon ground turmeric

1½ teaspoons garam masala (page 19)

1½ teaspoons salt

½ teaspoon chilli powder (optional)

125 g (4½ oz/½ cup) plain yoghurt

2 ripe tomatoes, diced

Joint the chicken (see page 10) and cut into serving pieces.

Put the onion, garlic, ginger, coriander and 60 ml (2 fl oz/¼ cup) water into a food processor and process to make a smooth purée. Heat the ghee in a heavy-based saucepan over medium heat and cook the onion mixture for about 5 minutes, stirring constantly. Add the turmeric, garam masala, salt and chilli powder, if using, and cook for a further 1 minute. Stir in the yoghurt and tomato, and cook until the liquid has been absorbed and the mixture is the consistency of a thick purée.

Add the chicken to the pan, turning to coat in the spice mixture, then reduce the heat to low, cover, and cook until the chicken is tender. If the liquid from the chicken has not evaporated by the time the flesh is cooked, uncover and increase the heat to dry it out, stirring gently at the base of the pan to prevent burning. Garnish with the extra coriander and serve with rice or Chapatis (page 23).

Murgh Tikka
Skewered barbecued chicken

Serves: 4–6

750 g (1 lb 11 oz) boneless skinless chicken breasts or thighs, cut into large cubes

1 onion, roughly chopped

1 garlic clove, sliced

2 teaspoons finely chopped fresh ginger

2 tablespoons lemon juice

1 teaspoon ground coriander

½ teaspoon ground cumin

1 teaspoon garam masala (page 19)

60 g (2 oz/¼ cup) plain yoghurt

1 teaspoon salt

Soak 8–12 bamboo skewers in water to prevent them from burning during cooking.

Put the onion, garlic and ginger into a food processor and process to a purée, adding the lemon juice if required. Transfer to a bowl and stir in the coriander, cumin, garam masala, yoghurt and salt. Add the chicken and toss to coat. Leave to marinate for 2 hours at room temperature or longer in the refrigerator.

Thread the chicken pieces onto the bamboo skewers and cook over glowing coals or under a preheated grill (broiler) until cooked through. Serve with Onion sambal (page 159) and Puris (page 26) or Chapatis (page 23).

Moglai Murgh
Chicken, Moghul-style

Serves: 6

1.5 kg (3 lb 5 oz) whole chicken

3 garlic cloves, crushed

1 teaspoon finely grated fresh ginger

1 teaspoon ground turmeric

½ teaspoon saffron strands

60 ml (2 fl oz/¼ cup) boiling milk

3 tablespoons ghee or oil

2 large onions, thinly sliced

2 teaspoons No. 1 garam masala (page 19)

1 teaspoon No. 2 garam masala with
   fragrant spices (page 24)

2 teaspoons salt

2 tablespoons ground almonds

125 ml (4 fl oz/½ cup) pouring
   (single/light) cream

2 tablespoons chopped fresh coriander
   (cilantro) leaves

Joint the chicken (see page 10) and cut into serving pieces.

Combine the garlic, ginger and turmeric and rub all over the chicken to coat.

Soak the saffron strands in the boiling milk for 10 minutes.

Heat the ghee in a large heavy-based frying pan over medium heat. Add the onion and cook until golden brown, then remove to a plate. Add the chicken and brown lightly on all sides. Sprinkle over both kinds of garam masala and the salt, then add the saffron milk, half of the cooked onion and 125 ml (4 fl oz/½ cup) hot water. Cover and cook until the chicken is tender, turning halfway through cooking.

Remove the chicken to a warm serving plate using a slotted spoon. Add the almonds and cream to the liquid in the pan and heat through, stirring well. Spoon the sauce over the chicken and serve, garnished with the remaining onion and the coriander. Serve hot with rice or Chapatis (page 23).

Dhansak
Chicken or lamb with lentils

Serves: 8–10

A Parsi dish, dhansak is served every Sunday in many Parsi homes and plays an important part at festive meals. The list of ingredients looks formidable, but the recipe consists of just five parts – meat or chicken, lentils, vegetables, a blended masala and a dry masala. This dish is served with rice, onion kachumbar and other accompaniments, and is a very hearty and filling meal.

220 g (8 oz/1 cup) yellow split peas

110 g (4 oz/½ cup) dried chickpeas (garbanzo beans)

110 g (4 oz/½ cup) moong dal (split dried mung beans)

125 g (4½ oz/½ cup) red lentils

2 kg (4 lb 6 oz) whole chicken or 1.5 kg (3 lb 5 oz) lamb shoulder, boned

1 tablespoon salt

1 eggplant (aubergine), chopped

1 slice of pumpkin (winter squash), peeled and chopped

1 large potato, peeled and chopped

2 onions, chopped, plus 4 onions, thinly sliced, extra

2 ripe tomatoes, peeled and chopped

100 g (3½ oz/2 cups) English spinach leaves, chopped

1–3 tablespoons ghee or oil

Blended masala

6 dry red chillies, deseeded

6 fresh green chillies, deseeded

1 tablespoon finely chopped fresh ginger

10 garlic cloves, peeled

15 g (½ oz/½ cup) fresh mint leaves

15 g (½ oz/½ cup) fresh coriander (cilantro) leaves

Dry ground masala

1 tablespoon ground coriander

2 teaspoons ground cumin

2 teaspoons ground turmeric

½ teaspoon ground cinnamon

½ teaspoon ground cardamom

½ teaspoon freshly ground black pepper

½ teaspoon black mustard seeds, bruised

¼ teaspoon ground fenugreek

¼ teaspoon ground cloves

Rinse the split peas, chickpeas, moong dal and red lentils separately and soak in separate bowls overnight. Drain well.

Joint the chicken (see page 10) and cut into serving pieces, or cut the lamb into large cubes.

Place the meat in a large saucepan with the split peas, chickpeas, moong dal and lentils and pour in enough water to cover. Add the salt and bring to the boil, then reduce the heat to low, cover, and simmer for 15 minutes. Add the eggplant, pumpkin, potato, chopped onion, tomato and spinach and continue cooking for 30 minutes, or until the meat is almost cooked. Remove the meat to a plate. Put all the lentils and vegetables in a food processor and process to a smooth purée.

To make the blended masala, put all the ingredients into a food processor with 60 ml (2 fl oz/¼ cup) hot water and process to a smooth paste.

To make the dry ground masala, combine all the ingredients in a bowl and stir well to combine.

Heat the ghee in a large saucepan over low heat. Add the sliced onion and cook, stirring frequently, until the onions are brown. Remove to a plate. Add the blended masala and the dry ground masala to the pan at the same time and cook, stirring constantly, until they are well cooked and give out a pleasing aroma. Add half of the reserved onion, the meat and the vegetable purée. Bring to the boil, then reduce the heat to low and simmer for 20–30 minutes. Season with salt and serve garnished with the remaining onion.

Buhari Murgh
Spiced deep-fried chicken

Serves: 4

Named in honour of a favourite Muslim restaurant, where the fried chicken was like no other fried chicken we have ever tasted, this recipe evolved out of a nostalgic determination to try to duplicate the original.

2 × 500 g (1 lb 2 oz) spatchcocks (poussin/ Cornish game hens)

3 spring onions (scallions), roughly chopped

4 garlic cloves, peeled

2 teaspoons finely chopped fresh ginger

2 tablespoons lemon juice

2 tablespoons chopped fresh coriander (cilantro) leaves

2 teaspoons sesame oil

2 teaspoons peanut oil

2 teaspoons ground coriander

1 teaspoon ground cumin

1 teaspoon paprika

½ teaspoon chilli powder

1½ teaspoons salt

oil for frying

Cut each spatchcock in half, lengthways.

Put the onion, garlic, ginger, lemon juice, chopped coriander and sesame and peanut oils into a food processor and process to a smooth purée. Add the ground spices and salt and process briefly to combine. Rub the spice mixture over the spatchcock halves, cover and refrigerate overnight.

Put the spatchcocks on a deep plate and steam for 30 minutes over a pan of simmering water. Pat dry with paper towel, being careful not to remove the spices.

Heat the oil in a large heavy-based saucepan over medium heat. When the oil is hot, deep-fry the spatchcocks for 2 minutes, or until brown all over. Serve with spiced pilau rice and Onion sambal (page 159).

Note

Any juices that collect in the plate when steaming the spatchcocks can be added to the liquid when cooking the rice.

Tandoori Murgh
Spiced roast chicken

Serves: 4

Tandoori chicken, perhaps the most well-known of all Indian chicken preparations, takes its name from the tandoor or clay oven in which it is cooked. Shaped like one of Ali Baba's jars and usually buried in earth, the tandoor is heated by white-hot coals within. The chicken is threaded on a very long skewer, which is lowered into the oven, leaving the bird to cook over the coals. Try this version cooked in a gas or electric oven – it does not have the same flavour as when cooked over coals, but is too delicious to miss.

2 × 500 g (1 lb 2 oz) skinless spatchcocks (poussin/Cornish game hens)

½ teaspoon saffron strands

1 tablespoon boiling water

4 garlic cloves, peeled

1 tablespoon finely chopped fresh ginger

1 tablespoon lemon juice

½ teaspoon chilli powder

1 teaspoon paprika

1½ teaspoons garam masala (page 19)

2 teaspoons salt

40 g (1½ oz) ghee

Note

If the oven has a rotisserie, it is ideal for cooking tandoori chicken, but it will still be necessary to baste the birds because the skin has been removed.

Make slits in the flesh of the spatchcock thighs, drumsticks and breasts, to allow the spices to penetrate. Dry the spatchcocks with paper towel.

Gently heat the saffron strands in a frying pan over low heat for 1–2 minutes, shaking the pan frequently to make sure they don't burn. Remove to a plate to cool and crisp, then crush to a powder in a cup, adding the boiling water to dissolve.

Put the saffron water into a food processor with the garlic, ginger and lemon juice and process until smooth. Transfer to a bowl and add all the remaining ingredients except the ghee, stirring well to combine.

Rub the spice mixture all over the spatchcocks, especially in the slits made in the flesh. Cover and leave to marinate for 2 hours at least, or preferably refrigerate overnight.

Preheat the oven to 200°C (400°F). Put the ghee in a roasting tin and heat in the oven for a minute to melt the ghee, then spread over the base of the tin. Put the spatchcocks in the roasting tin, breast side down, so they are side by side but not touching. Spoon the melted ghee over the birds then roast for 20 minutes. Baste with ghee, turn on one side and roast for 15 minutes. Baste again, then turn to cook the other side for a further 15 minutes. Turn the spatchcocks, breast side up, baste well with ghee and pan juices, and cook for a further 10–15 minutes, basting every 5 minutes. Serve hot with Paratha (page 28) or Naan (page 30) and an onion salad.

Badhak Vindaloo
Hot and sour curry of duck

Serves: 4

2.5 kg (5 lb) whole duck

6–10 dried red chillies, deseeded

125 ml (4 fl oz/½ cup) vinegar

6 garlic cloves

1 tablespoon finely chopped fresh ginger

1 tablespoon ground coriander

2 teaspoons ground cumin

1 teaspoon ground turmeric

½ teaspoon freshly ground black pepper

2 tablespoons ghee or oil

2 teaspoons salt

1 tablespoon sugar

Wash the duck and pat dry with paper towel. Cut the duck into serving pieces.

Soak the dried chillies in the vinegar for 5–10 minutes. Put the chillies, vinegar, garlic and ginger into a food processor and process until smooth.

Transfer the chilli mixture to a large bowl and stir in the ground spices and pepper. Add the duck and turn to coat all over. Cover and leave to marinate for 2 hours or overnight in the refrigerator.

Heat the ghee in a large heavy-based frying pan over medium heat. Add the duck and marinade, salt and a little hot water. Reduce the heat to low, cover, and simmer for 1½–2 hours, or until the duck is tender, stirring occasionally and turning the duck so that it does not stick in the pan or burn. Add more water if necessary during cooking. At the end of the cooking time, stir in the sugar until dissolved. Serve with rice.

Chicken Everest
Spiced roasted chicken

Serves: 6

My husband, Reuben, was a wonderful clarinetist with a flair for improvisation. That talent was apparent when he cooked, too. Here is one of his most successful variations on a traditional Indian theme, which accounts for the lack of an Indian name – and the presence of soy sauce (shock, horror!). Using ground rice in the marinade gives the chicken a wonderfully crisp coating.

1.5 kg (3 lb 5 oz) whole chicken

2 garlic cloves, crushed

2 teaspoons finely grated fresh ginger

1½ tablespoons Indian curry powder

1 teaspoon paprika

2 teaspoons salt

½ teaspoon freshly ground black pepper

1 teaspoon garam masala (page 19)

1 teaspoon amchur powder or 2 tablespoons lemon juice

½ teaspoon ground curry leaves

2 teaspoons light soy sauce

2 tablespoons oil

2 tablespoons ground rice

2 tablespoons finely chopped spring onions (scallions)

2 tablespoons chopped fresh coriander (cilantro) leaves

Wipe the chicken inside and out with damp paper towel.

Combine all the other ingredients with just enough warm water to make a paste of spreading consistency.

Rub the spice paste inside and outside the chicken. Set aside for at least 1 hour to marinate.

Preheat the oven to 170°C (340°F). Place the chicken in a roasting tin and roast for 1–1¼ hours, or until the juices run clear when pierced with a knife. If the chicken browns too much during cooking, cover with foil. Serve the chicken warm or cold with rice, bread or a salad.

Badhak Buffado

Spiced duck with cabbage and potatoes

Serves: 4–5

2.5 kg (5½ lb) whole duck

2 tablespoons oil

1 large onion, sliced

4 whole cloves

4 cardamom pods

1 cinnamon stick

1 teaspoon finely grated fresh ginger

1 teaspoon ground turmeric

½ teaspoon freshly ground black pepper

2 teaspoons ground coriander

2 fresh red or green chillies

2 teaspoons salt

2 tablespoons vinegar

4 potatoes, peeled

½ head cabbage, cut into wedges

155 g (5½ oz/1 cup) fresh or frozen peas

Wash the duck and pat dry with paper towel. Cut the duck into serving pieces.

Heat the oil in a large heavy-based saucepan over medium heat. Add the onion and whole spices and cook until the onion is golden. Add the ginger, turmeric, pepper and coriander and cook for a further 1–2 minutes, then add the duck and cook, turning often, until the duck is lightly browned all over.

Add the whole chillies to the pan (deseed them if a less hot flavour is preferred), with the salt, vinegar and 500 ml (17 fl oz/2 cups) hot water. Cover and simmer for 45 minutes, or until the duck is almost tender, skimming the surface occasionally to remove any excess fat. Add the potatoes and cook for 10 minutes, then add the cabbage and cook for a further 10 minutes. Finally, add the peas, adjust the seasoning if necessary, cover, and cook until the peas are done. Serve hot.

Meats

*

Goani Kebab
Goanese kebab curry

Serves: 6

500 g (1 lb 2 oz) lean lamb

500 g (1 lb 2 oz) pork neck or scotch fillet

thin slices fresh ginger

2 tablespoons ghee or oil

1 large onion, finely chopped

4 garlic cloves, finely chopped

2 fresh red or green chillies, deseeded

1 tablespoon ground cumin

2 tablespoons black mustard seeds, ground

2 teaspoons chilli powder, or to taste

2 teaspoons garam masala (page 19)

125 ml (4 fl oz/½ cup) vinegar

2 teaspoons salt

½ teaspoon freshly ground black pepper

Soak 6 bamboo skewers in water to prevent them from burning during cooking.

Trim the lamb and pork of any excess fat and cut into large cubes. Thread the meats alternately with the ginger slices onto the skewers.

Heat the ghee in a large heavy-based frying pan over medium heat. Add the onion, garlic and chilli and cook until the onion softens and turns golden brown. Add the ground spices and garam masala and continue stirring for 1 minute. Add the vinegar, salt, pepper and 125 ml (4 fl oz/½ cup) water and bring to the boil. Add the lamb skewers, turning to coat in the spice mixture, then cover and cook over low heat until the meat is tender – turn the kebabs once or twice during cooking. When the meat is tender, cook uncovered until the sauce has thickened and darkened. Serve hot with rice and accompaniments.

Meats

Korma
Lamb with spices and yoghurt

Serves: 6

I have noticed that commercial kormas can be quite sweet, although traditionally this is not so. Whether this is to pander to Western taste buds, I'm not sure. If that is your preference, add a couple of teaspoons of sugar at the end of cooking.

1 kg (2 lb 3 oz) boned leg of lamb

2 onions

1 tablespoon finely chopped fresh ginger

2 large garlic cloves

40 g (1½ oz/¼ cup) raw cashew nuts or blanched almonds

2–6 dried red chillies, deseeded

2 teaspoons ground coriander

1 teaspoon ground cumin

¼ teaspoon ground cinnamon

¼ teaspoon ground cardamom

¼ teaspoon ground cloves

½ teaspoon saffron strands

2 tablespoons boiling water

20 g (¾ oz) ghee

2 tablespoons oil

2 teaspoons salt

125 g (4½ oz/½ cup) plain yoghurt

2 tablespoons chopped fresh coriander (cilantro) leaves

Cut the lamb into large cubes, trimming off any excess fat.

Peel the onions; slice one thinly and set aside. Finely chop the other onion and place in a food processor with the ginger, garlic, cashew nuts and chillies. Add 125 ml (4 fl oz/½ cup) water and process to make a smooth paste. Add all the ground spices and process until well combined.

Put the saffron strands into a small bowl with the boiling water and allow to soak while cooking the masala.

Heat the ghee and oil in a large saucepan over low heat. Add the sliced onion and cook, stirring frequently with a wooden spoon, until soft and golden. Add the spice mixture and continue to cook, stirring constantly until the oil starts to separate. Add 60 ml (2 fl oz/¼ cup) water to the pan together with the salt and continue to stir until the liquid evaporates. Add the lamb and stir over medium heat until each piece is coated with the spice. Stir the saffron, crushing the strands against the side of the bowl, then add to the pan and stir to combine. Add the yoghurt and stir again until mixed through.

Reduce the heat to low, cover, and simmer for 1 hour, or until the lamb is tender and the sauce has thickened. Make sure you stir occasionally, taking care that the spice mixture does not stick to the base of the pan. When the lamb is cooked, sprinkle with the coriander leaves, replace the lid and cook for 5 minutes further. Serve the lamb korma hot with rice.

Mutton Kari
Lamb curry

Serves: 6–8

This is curry in its simplest form, using commercial curry powder – make sure it is fresh and of good quality.

2 tablespoons ghee or oil

2 large onions, chopped

4 garlic cloves, chopped

1 tablespoon finely chopped fresh ginger

2 tablespoons Indian curry powder

3 teaspoons salt

2 tablespoons vinegar or lemon juice

1.5 kg (3 lb 5 oz) boned shoulder of lamb,
   cut into 5 cm (2 in) cubes

3 large tomatoes, chopped

2 fresh red chillies, deseeded and sliced

2 tablespoons chopped fresh mint leaves

1 teaspoon garam masala (page 19)

1 tablespoon chopped fresh coriander
   (cilantro) leaves

Heat the ghee in a saucepan over low heat. Add the onion, garlic and ginger and cook until the onion is golden. Add the curry powder, salt and vinegar and stir thoroughly. Add the lamb and cook, stirring constantly, until the lamb is coated with the spice mixture. Add the tomato, chilli and mint, cover, and cook over low heat for 1¼ hours, stirring occasionally, until the lamb is tender – the tomatoes should provide enough liquid for the meat to cook in but, if necessary, add up to 125 ml (4 fl oz/½ cup) hot water to prevent the meat sticking to the pan. Add the garam masala and coriander for the last 5 minutes of cooking time. Serve hot.

Note

You can substitute goat for lamb, if preferred.

Seekh Botee
Skewered mutton curry

Serves: 4–6

1 kg (2 lb 3 oz) boned leg of lamb or mutton, cut into cubes

about 30 thin slices of fresh young ginger

3 tablespoons ghee or oil

1 large onion, finely chopped

3 garlic cloves, finely chopped

1 tablespoon ground coriander

2 teaspoons ground cumin

½ teaspoon ground fennel

½ teaspoon ground turmeric

½ teaspoon freshly ground black pepper

2 teaspoons salt

1 ripe tomato, diced

2 fresh green chillies, deseeded and sliced

½ teaspoon ground cinnamon

½ teaspoon ground cardamom

¼ teaspoon ground cloves

Soak 8 long or 16 short bamboo skewers in water to prevent them from burning during cooking. Thread the lamb cubes on the bamboo skewers, alternating each piece of meat with a thin slice of ginger. Cut the ginger from a slender root so the slices will not be too big, or cut large slices in pieces.

Heat the ghee in a large frying pan over medium–low heat and cook the onion until it softens, stirring occasionally. Add the garlic and continue cooking until the onion is golden brown. Add the coriander, cumin, fennel, turmeric and pepper and cook for 1 minute, then add the salt and tomato and cook for a further 3 minutes. Add the chilli and skewered meat and fry until the meat is lightly browned. Reduce the heat, cover, and cook until the meat is tender and the sauce has thickened – stir occasionally to prevent the spices catching on the base of the pan. About 10 minutes before the end of the cooking time sprinkle in the cinnamon, cardamom and cloves and stir well. Serve hot with rice and accompaniments.

Keema Mattar Pilau
Minced meat and peas with rice

Serves: 6

A wholesome one-dish meal, needing only pickles, sambal or raita as an accompaniment.

400 g (14 oz/2 cups) long-grain rice

3 tablespoons ghee or oil

1 teaspoon cumin seeds

1 onion, finely chopped

1 garlic clove, crushed

½ teaspoon finely grated fresh ginger

6 whole cloves

250 g (9 oz) minced (ground) lamb or beef

310 g (10½ oz/2 cups) fresh or frozen green peas

3 teaspoons salt

1 teaspoon garam masala (page 19)

Wash the rice well and drain in a colander for 30 minutes.

Heat the ghee in a large heavy-based saucepan over low heat. Add the cumin, onion, garlic, ginger and whole cloves and cook until the onion is soft and golden brown.

Add the mince to the pan and cook over medium–high heat until the meat has browned, breaking up any large lumps with a fork. Add the peas and 125 ml (4 fl oz/½ cup) hot water and stir well, then cover and cook until the peas are just tender. Add the rice and 875 ml (29½ fl oz/3½ cups) hot water and stir in the salt. Bring to the boil, then reduce the heat to low, cover, and cook for 10 minutes. Uncover and sprinkle with garam masala but do not stir. Replace the lid and continue cooking for a further 10 minutes, or until all the liquid has been absorbed and the rice is cooked through. Serve hot.

Korma Pilau
Rice with spiced lamb in yoghurt

Serves: 6–8

¼ teaspoon saffron strands

190 ml (6½ fl oz/¾ cup) hot milk

2 tablespoons rosewater

3 drops kewra essence (optional) (glossary)

40 g (1½ oz) ghee

1 quantity lamb korma (page 104)

1 quantity Yakhni pilau (page 41) using
lamb stock or water in place of chicken
and cooking the rice for 15 minutes only

1 ripe tomato, thinly sliced, to serve

1 cucumber, thinly sliced, to serve

1 onion, thinly sliced, to serve

2 fresh green chillies, deseeded and thinly
sliced, to serve

3 hard-boiled eggs, peeled and sliced or
quartered, to serve

3 tablespoons slivered almonds, toasted,
to serve

Soak the saffron strands in the hot milk and press to diffuse as much of the colour as possible. Stir in the rosewater and kewra essence, if using.

Preheat the oven to 150°C (300°F). Grease a large ovenproof casserole dish with the ghee and arrange the lamb korma and pilau in layers. Sprinkle each layer of pilau with the saffron and milk mixture. Finish with a layer of pilau. Cover the casserole and cook in the oven for 30 minutes.

Garnish the top of the korma pilau with the remaining ingredients and serve hot.

Note

Alternatively, you can cook the pilau for 20 minutes. Remove two-thirds of the pilau from the pan in which it was cooked, sprinkle the pilau in the pan with one-third of the saffron milk mixture and add half of the lamb korma, spreading it to the sides of the pan. Cover with half the pilau, sprinkle the pilau with half of the remaining milk. Make a layer of the remaining korma and cover that with the rest of the pilau. Sprinkle the remaining milk over the top, cover, and cook over low heat for 25–30 minutes.

Kashmiri Roghan Josh
Lamb in yoghurt and spices, Kashmiri–style

Serves: 6

Asafoetida is mixed with rice flour, but if you have the pure resin, much less is required to deliver the desired flavour to a dish.

⅛ teaspoon asafoetida (optional)

125 g (4½ oz/½ cup) plain yoghurt

40 g (1½ oz) ghee

2 teaspoons salt

1 teaspoon ground ginger

1 kg (2 lb 6 oz) boned leg of lamb, cut into 5 cm (2 in) cubes

1 teaspoon chilli powder, or to taste

1 tablespoon finely grated fresh ginger

2 teaspoons Kashmiri garam masala (page 24)

2 tablespoons chopped fresh coriander (cilantro) leaves

Combine the asafoetida, if using, with 1 tablespoon of hot water and stir to dissolve. Add the yoghurt, ghee, salt and ground ginger and mix well to combine.

Place the yoghurt mixture in a large heavy-based saucepan with the lamb over low heat. Cover and cook, stirring regularly, until the juices given out by the lamb evaporate and the spice mixture starts to stick to the base of pan. Add 125 ml (4 fl oz/½ cup) hot water, the chilli powder and fresh ginger and stir well with the wooden spoon, scraping the dried mixture from the base of the pan and incorporating it with the liquid added. Continue to cook, covered, until the liquid evaporates and the mixture sticks to the pan.

Add 375 ml (12½ fl oz/1½ cups) hot water to the pan and continue cooking this way until the meat is very tender, adding no more than 125 ml (4 fl oz/½ cup) water at a time. Sprinkle over the garam masala and coriander, cover and cook for a further 10–15 minutes. Serve hot with rice, Chapatis (page 23) or Paratha (page 28).

Roghan Josh
Lamb in spices and yoghurt

Serves: 6

3 dried red chillies, deseeded

6–8 garlic cloves

1 tablespoon finely chopped fresh ginger

2 tablespoons desiccated (shredded) coconut, toasted

2 tablespoons blanched almonds

1 tablespoon ground coriander

1 teaspoon ground cumin

1 teaspoon poppy seeds

½ teaspoon ground fennel

½ teaspoon ground cardamom

¼ teaspoon ground cloves

¼ teaspoon ground mace

½ teaspoon freshly ground black pepper

3 tablespoons ghee or oil

1 onion, finely chopped

4 cardamom pods, bruised

½ teaspoon ground turmeric

125 g (4½ oz/½ cup) plain yoghurt

2 ripe tomatoes, peeled and chopped

1½ teaspoons salt

750 g (1 lb 11 oz) lean boned leg or shoulder of lamb, cut into 5 cm (2 in) cubes

1 teaspoon garam masala (page 19)

2 tablespoons chopped fresh coriander (cilantro) leaves

Soak the chillies in 125 ml (4 fl oz/½ cup) hot water for 5 minutes. Drain well, reserving 2 tablespoons of the soaking liquid.

Put the garlic, ginger, coconut, almonds and chilli in a food processor with the reserved soaking liquid and process to make a smooth paste.

Put the ground coriander, cumin, poppy seeds and fennel in a small frying pan and shake over low heat for a few minutes until the spices become aromatic. Add to the chilli paste and continue to process until well combined and smooth. Remove from the food processor container to a bowl and stir through the cardamom, cloves, mace and pepper. Set aside.

Heat the ghee in a large heavy-based saucepan over low heat. Add the onion and cook, stirring regularly, until the onion is golden brown. Add the cardamom pods, turmeric and chilli paste and cook until the ghee starts to separate from the spices. Add the yoghurt, a spoonful at a time, and stir to combine. Add the tomato and salt, and cook for a further 5 minutes, then add the lamb and cook over high heat, stirring and turning the meat so that each piece is well coated. Reduce the heat to low, cover, and cook for 1 hour or longer – the lamb should be very tender and the liquid almost absorbed. Stir occasionally to ensure that the spices don't stick to the base of the pan.

Sprinkle the garam masala over the top, replace the lid and cook for a further 5 minutes. Sprinkle with the coriander leaves and serve immediately with plain rice or a pilau.

Badami Gosht
Spiced lamb with saffron and almonds

Serves: 6–8

½ teaspoon saffron strands

60 ml (2 fl oz/¼ cup) boiling water

3 teaspoons salt

250 g (9 oz/1 cup) plain yoghurt

1.5 kg (3 lb 5 oz) boned leg of lamb, cut into
    5 cm (2 in) cubes

40 g (1½ oz) ghee

2 tablespoons oil

1 cinnamon stick

6 cardamom pods, bruised

6 whole cloves

1 large onion, finely chopped

4 garlic cloves, finely chopped

2 teaspoons finely grated fresh ginger

2 teaspoons ground cumin

2 tablespoons ground almonds

1 tablespoon chopped fresh mint (optional)

Soak the saffron strands in the boiling water for 10 minutes. Stir together the saffron water, salt and yoghurt in a large bowl, then add the lamb and toss to coat. Cover and set aside to marinate while preparing the remaining ingredients.

Heat the ghee and oil in a large heavy-based saucepan over medium heat. Add the cinnamon stick, cardamom pods and cloves and cook for 1–2 minutes, then add the onion, garlic and ginger and continue cooking for about 10 minutes, or until the onion is soft and golden. Add the cumin and stir to combine.

Drain the lamb from the yoghurt marinade and add to the pan, turning to brown on all sides. Add the marinade and ground almonds. Mix any remaining marinade with 125 ml (4 fl oz/½ cup) water and add to the pan. Reduce the heat to low, cover, and cook for 1 hour, or until the lamb is tender and the sauce has thickened. Towards the end of cooking stir with a wooden spoon to ensure it doesn't stick to the base of the pan. Sprinkle with mint, if using, cover, and cook for a further 5 minutes. Serve hot with rice. A light, slightly sweet rice dish such as Parsi pilau (page 37) goes particularly well with this.

Raan
Roast leg of lamb with Kashmiri spices

Serves: 8

2.5 kg (5½ lb) boned leg of lamb, trimmed
  of excess fat

1 tablespoon finely grated fresh ginger

4 garlic cloves, crushed

3 teaspoons salt

1 teaspoon ground cumin

1 teaspoon ground turmeric

½ teaspoon freshly ground black pepper

½ teaspoon ground cinnamon

½ teaspoon ground cardamom

¼ teaspoon ground cloves

½ teaspoon chilli powder (optional)

2 tablespoons lemon juice

½ teaspoon saffron strands

2 tablespoons boiling water

185 g (6½ oz/¾ cup) plain yoghurt

2 tablespoons blanched almonds

2 tablespoons pistachio nuts

3 teaspoons honey

Using a sharp knife make short deep slits all over the lamb.

Combine the ginger, garlic, salt, ground spices and lemon juice and rub all over the lamb, pressing into each cut – if the mixture is too dry to spread, add a little oil.

Soak the saffron strands in a bowl with the boiling water for 10 minutes. Place in a food processor with the yoghurt, almonds and pistachio nuts and process until smooth. Spoon the purée over the lamb, then drizzle over the honey. Cover and set aside to marinate at least overnight in the refrigerator, or 2 days if possible.

Preheat the oven to 230°C (445°F). Put the lamb in a casserole dish, cover, and cook for 30 minutes, then reduce the oven temperature to 170°C (340°F) and cook for a further 1¾ hours, or until the lamb is cooked through. Uncover the lamb and cool to room temperature. Serve with Namkin chawal (page 33).

Qabargah or Kamargah
Lamb chops in spicy batter

Serves: 4

This is a Kashmiri method of preparing lamb – first it is simmered in milk and spices, then fried in batter.

8 small lamb chops or cutlets

375 ml (12½ fl oz/1½ cups) milk

1 teaspoon salt

8 cardamom pods, bruised

8 whole cloves

1 cinnamon stick

½ teaspoon whole black peppercorns

2 teaspoons melted ghee or oil

Batter

35 g (1¼ oz/⅓ cup) besan (chickpea flour)

1 teaspoon ground coriander

½ teaspoon salt

¼ teaspoon ground cardamom

¼ teaspoon chilli powder

a pinch each of ground cinnamon, nutmeg,
  cloves and turmeric

Put the lamb chops in a saucepan with the milk, salt, cardamom pods, cloves, cinnamon stick, peppercorns and 125 ml (4 fl oz/½ cup) water and bring to the boil. Reduce the heat to low and simmer, covered, until the meat is tender and the liquid evaporates. Remove from the heat and allow to cool while preparing the batter.

To make the batter, mix all the ingredients together in a bowl with 80 ml (2½ fl oz/⅓ cup) water, beating with a wooden spoon until smooth. Let stand for 30 minutes.

Heat the ghee in a large heavy-based frying pan over medium heat. Dip each lamb chop into the batter, coating them all over, then gently lower into the hot oil and fry until golden brown on both sides. Drain well on paper towel. Repeat until all are cooked, then serve hot with Indian breads and vegetables.

Lamb Kebabs

Serves: 6–8

Let me confess that this is not a traditional Indian recipe – no Indian cook would use oregano or soy sauce. It evolved when I was in an unorthodox mood, and proved so delicious that I wrote it down and have used it frequently. Strangely enough, the kebabs still have an Indian flavour.

2 kg (4 lb 6 oz) boned leg of lamb

1 large garlic clove

2 teaspoons salt

1½ teaspoons finely grated fresh ginger

1 teaspoon freshly ground black pepper

1 teaspoon ground turmeric

1 teaspoon ground coriander

1 teaspoon ground cumin

1 teaspoon crushed dried curry leaves

1 teaspoon crushed dried oregano leaves

1 tablespoon light soy sauce

1 tablespoon sesame oil

2 tablespoons peanut oil

1 tablespoon lemon juice

Trim the excess fat off the lamb, cut the meat into 2.5 cm (1 in) cubes and put it in a large bowl. Crush the garlic with the salt and combine in a bowl with the remaining ingredients, mixing well. Add the lamb and toss well to coat. Cover the bowl and refrigerate for at least 3 hours, or up to 4 days.

Thread the pieces of meat onto 6 metal skewers and cook under a hot grill (broiler) for about 5 minutes on each side. When nicely brown, serve hot with boiled rice or Parathas (page 28), accompanied by Onion sambal (page 159) and Mint chutney (page 166).

Meats

Keema Seekh Kebab
Minced meat on skewers

Serves: 4–6

500 g (1 lb 2 oz) minced (ground) lamb
   or beef

2 tablespoons besan (chickpea flour)

1 onion, finely chopped

1 garlic clove, crushed

2 tablespoons chopped fresh coriander
   (cilantro) leaves

1 teaspoon finely grated fresh ginger

1 teaspoon salt

1 teaspoon garam masala (page 19)

60 g (2 oz/¼ cup) plain yoghurt

Combine the minced meat with all the other ingredients except the yoghurt. Mix thoroughly and knead well until the mixture becomes very smooth. Form portions of the mixture into sausage shapes around six metal skewers. (Use skewers that are square or rectangular as the minced meat mixture will slip on round skewers.)

Beat the yoghurt slightly and coat the meat with it, then place over a preheated barbecue hotplate or under a hot grill (broiler) until browned on all sides and cooked through. Serve with rice or Indian bread, vegetables and other accompaniments.

Seekh Kebab Kari
Skewered lamb in spices

Serves: 4–6

These kebabs are marinated in a spice mixture and cooked in ghee before being simmered in curry.

750 g (1 lb 11 oz) boned shoulder of lamb

thin slices fresh young ginger

Marinade

2 teaspoons ground coriander

1 teaspoon garam masala (page 19)

1 teaspoon ground cumin

½ teaspoon ground ginger

½ teaspoon ground turmeric

⅛ teaspoon freshly grated nutmeg

4 garlic cloves, crushed

1 teaspoon salt

1 tablespoon oil

1 tablespoon lemon juice

Curry

3 tablespoons ghee or oil

1 onion, finely chopped

4 garlic cloves, crushed

1 cinnamon stick

4 cardamom pods, bruised

4 whole cloves

1 teaspoon chilli powder (optional)

½ teaspoon black cumin seeds, lightly toasted

½ teaspoon garam masala (page 24)

2 fresh green chillies, deseeded and sliced, to garnish

2 tablespoons chopped fresh coriander (cilantro) leaves to garnish

Soak 8–12 bamboo skewers in water to prevent them from burning during cooking.

Cut the lamb into 2.5 cm (1 in) cubes. Mix together all the marinade ingredients in a large bowl, adding more oil if necessary to make it a spreading consistency. Add the lamb and toss well to coat. Cover and set aside to marinate for at least 2 hours, or in the refrigerator overnight if possible.

Thread the lamb cubes onto the skewers alternately with the ginger slices. If the ginger has a very strong flavour, use fewer slices, say one slice of ginger to every 2 or 3 cubes of lamb.

To make the curry, heat the ghee in a large saucepan or frying pan over high heat. Add the lamb skewers, a few at a time, and cook until they are browned on all sides. Remove to a plate once cooked.

Reduce the heat to medium and cook the onion and garlic gently, stirring constantly, until they are golden brown. Add the whole spices and cook for a further 1 minute, then add the chilli powder, if using, and stir for a few seconds. Return the meat to the pan, add 125 ml (4 fl oz/½ cup) hot water, stir well to loosen any spices stuck on the base of the pan, cover, and simmer gently until the meat is tender and the sauce has reduced and thickened. Sprinkle over the cumin seeds and garam masala, stir to combine and heat through for a further 1 minute. Serve hot, garnished with the chilli and coriander, and with rice and accompaniments or Indian breads on the side.

Kashmiri Kofta Kari
Curried meatballs, Kashmiri-style

Serves: 6

A feature of Kashmiri Brahmin cooking is the absence of onions and garlic, both of which are supposed to inflame the baser passions. Kashmiri Brahmins also do not eat beef, so if this dish is to be made in the true Kashmiri tradition, use lamb instead.

750 g (1 lb 11 oz) lean minced (ground) lamb

1 teaspoon finely grated fresh ginger

2 fresh red chillies, deseeded and finely chopped, plus extra to garnish

1 teaspoon ground coriander

½ teaspoon chilli powder

2 teaspoons garam masala (page 19)

2 teaspoons salt

125 g (4½ oz/½ cup) plain yoghurt

60 g (2 oz) ghee

1 tablespoon dried milk or khoa (page 15)

1 teaspoon sugar

½ teaspoon freshly ground black pepper

¼ teaspoon ground cardamom

Put the lamb into a bowl with the ginger, chilli, coriander, chilli powder and 1 teaspoon each of the garam masala and salt, adding 1 tablespoon of the yoghurt to moisten the spices and help distribute them evenly. A teaspoon or so of the ghee can also be added if the lamb is very lean. Mix well and form into small oval shapes.

Heat the ghee in a large heavy-based saucepan over low heat. Add the dried milk, sugar, the remaining yoghurt and the garam masala and salt and stir well to heat through, then add 125 ml (4 fl oz/½ cup) hot water and bring to the boil. Add the koftas, reduce the heat to low and simmer, covered, until no liquid remains. Turn the koftas over, add another 125 ml (4 fl oz/½ cup) hot water and the pepper, cover, and simmer until all the liquid has been absorbed. Sprinkle over the cardamom, garnish with the extra chilli and serve with Indian breads or rice. (Cover after adding the cardamom so its fragrance will not dissipate.)

Botee Kebab
Mutton kebab

Serves: 6

500 g (1 lb 2 oz) mutton

2 tablespoons desiccated (shredded) coconut

1 large onion, roughly chopped

2 garlic cloves, peeled

1 teaspoon chopped fresh ginger

¼ teaspoon freshly grated nutmeg

¼ teaspoon ground cinnamon

¼ teaspoon ground cloves

¼ teaspoon ground cardamom

½ teaspoon freshly ground black pepper

1 teaspoon poppy seeds

125 g (4½ oz/½ cup) plain yoghurt

Soak 6 bamboo skewers in water to prevent them from burning during cooking.

Trim the mutton of excess fat but leave a thin layer, for it gives a delicious crisp layer when grilled (broiled). Cut the meat into bite-sized cubes. For Eastern cooking, meat is cut smaller than it is for Western-style kebabs. For one thing the flavours penetrate better; for another no knives are used at the table.

Toast the coconut in a dry frying pan over medium heat, stirring constantly, until golden brown. Set aside to cool.

Put the onion, garlic and ginger into a food processor and process to a smooth purée. Add the spices, toasted coconut, poppy seeds and yoghurt and process to combine – the coconut should be finely ground. Pour over the pieces of mutton in a large bowl and toss well to coat. Cover and set aside to marinate for at least 2 hours, or in the refrigerator overnight.

Thread the mutton cubes onto the skewers and cook under a preheated grill (broiler) or over glowing coals until brown all over and cooked through. Serve with Chapatis (page 23), Paratha (page 28) or rice, with Onion sambal (page 159).

Doh Piaza
Spiced lamb with onions

Serves: 8–10

The name of this dish translates literally as 'two onions', and it has never quite been settled whether this means the onions are added in two forms – raw and fried – or at two different stages of cooking. Or, that the dish has twice as much onion as most other preparations of this type.

1.5 kg (3 lb 5 oz) boned shoulder or leg of lamb or mutton

1 kg (2 lb 3 oz) onions

6 garlic cloves

1½ teaspoons finely grated fresh ginger

60 g (2 oz/¼ cup) plain yoghurt

1–2 teaspoons chilli powder, or to taste

1 teaspoon paprika

3 tablespoons chopped fresh coriander (cilantro) leaves

2 tablespoons ground coriander

2 teaspoons black cumin seeds

60 g (2 oz) ghee

60 ml (2 fl oz/¼ cup) oil

8 cardamom pods

1 teaspoon garam masala (page 19)

Trim the lamb of any excess fat and cut into large cubes.

Slice half the onions thinly and chop the rest. Put the chopped onions into a food processor with the garlic, ginger, yoghurt, chilli powder, paprika, coriander leaves, ground coriander and cumin seeds and process until smooth.

Heat the ghee and oil in a large heavy-based frying pan over medium heat. Add the sliced onion and cook, stirring often, until golden. Remove to a plate. Add the cubed meat to the pan, in batches, and cook over high heat until browned on all sides. Remove to a plate when cooked. Set aside.

Add a little more ghee or oil to the pan if needed, and cook the onion purée over medium heat, stirring constantly, until it becomes aromatic and oil starts to appear around the edges of the mixture.

Return the meat to the pan, add the cardamom pods, stir well, then cover and cook over low heat until the meat is almost tender, stirring occasionally. It might be necessary to add a little water, but usually the juices given out by the meat are sufficient. When the meat is tender and most of the liquid has been absorbed, add the garam masala and reserved fried onion, cover and continue to cook over low heat for a further 15 minutes. Serve the spiced lamb with rice or Indian breads.

Nargisi Kofta
Eggs in meatballs

Serves: 6

Named for their resemblance to the yellow and white flowers of the narcissus, these meatballs are fried, then simmered in curry and served as a main dish. For picnic fare try them just fried and served with a salad.

Meatballs

7 small eggs

500 g (1 lb 2 oz) twice-minced (ground) lamb or beef

1 small onion, finely chopped

2 garlic cloves, finely chopped

½ teaspoon finely grated fresh ginger

1 fresh green chilli, deseeded and finely chopped

1 teaspoon salt

1 teaspoon garam masala (page 19)

½ teaspoon ground turmeric

1½ tablespoons besan (chickpea flour)

1 tablespoon plain yoghurt

ghee or oil for frying

Curry

1 tablespoon ghee or oil

1 onion, finely chopped

5 garlic cloves, finely chopped

2 teaspoons finely grated fresh ginger

1 teaspoon garam masala (page 19)

1 teaspoon ground turmeric

½ teaspoon chilli powder

2 large ripe tomatoes

1 teaspoon salt

125 g (4½ oz/½ cup) plain yoghurt

2 tablespoons chopped fresh coriander (cilantro) leaves

Put 6 of the eggs into a saucepan of cold water and bring slowly to simmering point. Stir the eggs gently for the first 5 minutes to centre the yolks. Simmer for a further 10 minutes, then run cold water into the pan until the eggs are cold. Peel them and set aside.

Put the meat into a large heavy-based frying pan with the onion, garlic, ginger, chilli, salt, garam masala, turmeric and 125 ml (4 fl oz/½ cup) water. Stir well, bring to the boil, then cover and simmer for 20–30 minutes, or until the meat is well cooked. Stir in the besan and continue cooking until all the liquid has been absorbed. Remove from the heat and allow to cool, then knead the meat mixture with your hands until it is very smooth, adding a little yoghurt if necessary to moisten it.

Divide the meat into 6 equal portions and mould each one around one of the hard-boiled eggs. Beat the remaining egg in a bowl.

Heat the ghee in a large heavy-based saucepan over medium heat. Dip the koftas into the beaten egg, then gently lower into the hot oil and deep-fry until golden brown all over. Drain on paper towel. Cut each kofta in half using a sharp knife and serve with salad, or proceed with the next step to make curried meatballs.

To make the curry, heat the ghee in a large heavy-based frying pan over low heat. Add the onion and cook until soft and pale golden. Add the garlic and ginger and fry, stirring, until the onions are golden brown. Add the garam masala, turmeric and chilli powder, stir for a few seconds, then add the tomato and salt. Cover the pan and cook to a pulp, stirring occasionally. Mash the yoghurt until smooth, mix with 125 ml (4 fl oz/½ cup) hot water and add to the simmering curry. Stir well and cook uncovered until the sauce has thickened.

If the koftas are prepared beforehand they can be put into the sauce to heat through, then cut in halves and served with rice or Chapatis (page 23). Garnish with the fresh coriander leaves to serve.

Alu Chap

Spicy potato and savoury mince rissoles

Serves: 4

1 kg (2 lb 3 oz) potatoes, peeled and chopped

1 teaspoon salt

2 tablespoons finely chopped mint leaves

2 spring onions (scallions), finely chopped

1 fresh green chilli, deseeded and finely chopped

250 g (9 oz) Savoury mince filling (page 47)

oil for deep-frying

1 egg, lightly beaten

100 g (3½ oz/1 cup) dry breadcrumbs

Boil the potatoes in a saucepan of boiling water until tender, then mash until smooth. Mix in the salt, mint, spring onion and chilli and stir well to combine.

Divide the potato mixture into 8 or 10 even-sized portions and shape each into a flat circle. Place a spoonful of savoury mince filling in the centre of each and push the potato around it to enclose the meat so they resemble a thick round patty.

Heat the oil in a large heavy-based saucepan over medium heat. Dip each patty in the egg, then in the breadcrumbs, shaking off any excess. Gently lower the patties into the hot oil and deep-fry, in batches, until golden brown. Drain on paper towel. Serve hot with Mint chutney (page 166).

Keema Mattar
Minced meat with fresh peas

Serves: 4–6

40 g (1½ oz) ghee

1 large onion, thinly sliced

2 garlic cloves, crushed

½ teaspoon finely grated fresh ginger

1 teaspoon ground turmeric

½ teaspoon chilli powder

500 g (1 lb 2 oz) minced (ground) lamb
or goat

125 g (4½ oz/½ cup) plain yoghurt

155 g (5½ oz/1 cup) fresh or frozen
green peas

1 teaspoon garam masala (page 19)

1½ teaspoons salt

2 tablespoons finely chopped fresh
coriander (cilantro) leaves to garnish

1 fresh red chilli, deseeded and thinly
sliced, to garnish

Heat the ghee in a large heavy-based frying pan over low heat. Add the onion and cook until it softens. Add the garlic and ginger and cook until the onion is golden brown. Add the turmeric and chilli powder and stir for a few seconds, then add the mince and cook, turning the meat constantly to break up any large lumps, until it starts to brown. Stir in the yoghurt and peas, cover, and cook for 15 minutes. Add the garam masala and salt and continue cooking until the meat and peas are tender. Serve the minced meat garnished with the coriander leaves and chilli.

Keema Kari

Minced meat and split pea curry

Serves: 4–6

110 g (4 oz/½ cup) green or yellow split peas

2 tablespoons ghee or oil

2 onions, finely chopped

2 garlic cloves, finely chopped

1 teaspoon finely grated fresh ginger

1 teaspoon ground turmeric

½ teaspoon chilli powder

1 tablespoon chopped fresh coriander
(cilantro) or mint leaves

4 small ripe tomatoes, chopped

2 teaspoons salt

500 g (1 lb 2 oz) minced (ground) beef
or lamb

2 teaspoons garam masala (page 19)

Wash the split peas and soak in a bowl of water while preparing the other ingredients. Drain well.

Heat the ghee in a large heavy-based frying pan over medium heat. Add the onion, garlic and ginger and cook until soft. Add the turmeric, chilli powder, coriander, tomato and salt and stir over medium heat for a few minutes, then add the meat and drained split peas. Stir until well combined, then cover and simmer for 40 minutes, or until the meat and peas are tender, stirring from time to time (you may need to add a little water if the mixture becomes too dry).

Add the garam masala and cook until the liquid evaporates and the mixture fries in the fat left in the pan. At this stage stir frequently so it does not burn. Serve this dry curry with Indian bread and other accompaniments such as vegetable dishes, sambals and chutneys.

Shikar Vindaloo
Pork vindaloo

Serves: 6–8

Because of the high acid content of this recipe, cook it in an earthenware, enamel or stainless steel (non-reactive) vessel. Choose a cut of meat that suits your preference. Belly will be the fattiest.

1 kg (2 lb 6 oz) pork neck, belly or scotch fillet

6–8 large dried red chillies

250 ml (8½ fl oz/1 cup) vinegar

2 teaspoons finely chopped fresh ginger

7 garlic cloves

2 teaspoons ground cumin

½ teaspoon freshly ground black pepper

½ teaspoon ground cinnamon

½ teaspoon ground cardamom

¼ teaspoon ground cloves

¼ teaspoon freshly grated nutmeg

2 teaspoons salt

2–3 tablespoons ghee or oil

2 onions, finely chopped

1 tablespoon soft brown sugar (optional)

Trim the pork of any excess fat and cut into large cubes.

Soak the chillies in the vinegar for 10 minutes. Any kind of vinegar may be used, but if using double-strength cider vinegar dilute with an equal quantity of water. (Ideally, use coconut vinegar, which gives the correct flavour.)

Put the chillies and vinegar, ginger and garlic into a food processor and process until smooth. Stir through the ground spices and salt. Add the pork and toss to coat. Set aside to marinate for at least 2 hours.

Heat the ghee in a large heavy-based frying pan over medium heat. Add the onion and cook until soft and all the liquid from the onion has evaporated and the oil comes out. Drain the meat and add to the pan, turning often until the meat changes colour, then add the marinade, cover, and simmer over low heat until the meat is well cooked, about 1½ hours. Stir in the sugar, if using. Serve hot with rice and accompaniments.

Alu Gosht Kari
Meat and potato curry

Serves: 6–8

....

1.5 kg (3 lb 5 oz) skirt (flank) or other lean
  stewing steak

60 ml (2 fl oz/¼ cup) oil or 40 g (1½ oz) ghee

1 teaspoon black mustard seeds

½ teaspoon fenugreek seeds

6 garlic cloves, chopped

1 tablespoon finely chopped fresh ginger

3 onions, thinly sliced

1½ teaspoons ground turmeric

2 tablespoons ground coriander

1 tablespoon ground cumin

2 teaspoons chilli powder

3 teaspoons salt

80 ml (2½ fl oz/⅓ cup) vinegar

2 teaspoons garam masala (page 19)

750 g (1 lb 11 oz) potatoes, peeled and cubed

2 tablespoons chopped fresh coriander
  (cilantro) leaves

Trim the steak of any excess fat and cut into small cubes.

Heat the oil in a large saucepan over medium heat. Add the mustard seeds and cook until they start to pop. Add the fenugreek seeds, garlic, ginger and onion and cook over medium heat, stirring occasionally with a wooden spoon, until the onion just starts to brown. Add the turmeric and cook for 1 minute. Add the coriander, cumin and chilli powder and stir for a minute or so, then add the salt and 2 tablespoons of the vinegar and stir until the liquid dries up.

Sprinkle the garam masala into the pan and mix well, then add the steak, stirring to coat in the spices. If there is spice sticking to the base of the pan, add the remaining vinegar and stir, scraping as much as possible from the base of the pan. Reduce the heat, cover, and simmer for 1½–2 hours, or until the meat is tender – you may need to add a little water if the mixture becomes too dry. Add the potato, cover once more, and cook for 20–25 minutes, or until cooked through. Sprinkle with the coriander leaves and serve hot with rice or Indian bread.

Vegetables

*

Same Ka Bhaji
Spicy fried green beans

Serves: 4–6

Use any kind of beans, such as broad (fava) beans, French beans, string beans or snake (yard-long) beans – they all go well with this type of light spicing.

500 g (1 lb 2 oz) green beans

1 tablespoon ghee or oil

1 onion, finely chopped

½ teaspoon finely grated fresh ginger

1 teaspoon ground turmeric

1 teaspoon garam masala (page 19)

½ teaspoon chilli powder (optional)

2 teaspoons salt

2 ripe tomatoes, chopped or 60 ml
(2 fl oz/¼ cup) hot water

a squeeze of lemon juice

Trim the beans, remove the strings if needed, and cut them into bite-sized pieces.

Heat the ghee in a saucepan over medium–low heat and cook the onion and ginger until the onion is golden. Add the turmeric, garam masala, chilli powder and salt and cook for 2 minutes, stirring regularly. Add the tomato and stir-fry until the tomatoes are cooked to a pulp and most of the liquid evaporates. Add the beans and stir well, partially cover the pan, and cook until the beans are just tender – do not overcook. Stir in the lemon juice to taste and serve immediately.

Variation

You can make a drier version of this bean recipe by omitting the tomato and lemon juice – this makes the flavour less acidic.

Saag
Purée of leafy greens

Serves: 4–6

500 g (1 lb 2 oz) English spinach or other leafy greens

2 turnips or 1 large daikon (white radish), peeled and diced

1 tablespoon ghee or oil

½ teaspoon black mustard seeds or panch phora (page 15)

1 onion, finely chopped

1 teaspoon finely grated fresh ginger

½ teaspoon chilli powder

½ teaspoon ground turmeric

1½ teaspoons salt, or to taste

½ teaspoon garam masala (page 19)

lemon juice to taste (optional)

Wash the greens, removing any tough stalks. Break the leaves into small pieces and place into a large saucepan with a sprinkling of water. Add the turnip to the pan, cover and cook over low heat until the vegetables soften. Drain any liquid from the pan, then chop or mash the vegetables together.

Heat the ghee in a frying pan over medium heat and cook the mustard seeds or panch phora for 1 minute, then add the onion and ginger and cook until the onion is soft and golden. Add the chilli powder, turmeric, salt and mashed vegetables, stir well and cook for 5 minutes. Sprinkle with the garam masala, cover, and leave on low heat for a few minutes longer until all the liquid evaporates. Taste and season with salt or lemon juice, if desired. Serve with Chapatis (page 23) or rice and curries.

Sukhe Phalli Kari
Curried dried beans

Serves: 4

Make this curry with Bengal peas, chickpeas (garbanzo beans), cannellini (lima) beans, butterbeans or any favourite variety of dried beans.

250 g (9 oz) dried beans

2 teaspoons salt

1½ tablespoons ghee or oil

1 large onion, finely chopped

2 garlic cloves, finely chopped

1 tablespoon finely chopped fresh ginger

1 teaspoon ground turmeric

1 teaspoon garam masala (page 19)

2 large ripe tomatoes, chopped

1–2 fresh green chillies, deseeded and chopped

2 tablespoons chopped fresh mint

2 tablespoons lemon juice

Put the dried beans in a bowl with enough water to cover and leave to soak overnight. Rinse well and drain.

Put the beans into a large saucepan with enough fresh water to cover and add 1 teaspoon of the salt. Bring to the boil, cover, and cook until tender. Add more hot water during cooking if needed, to keep the beans submerged. Drain and reserve the cooking liquid.

Heat the ghee in a large saucepan over medium heat. Add the onion, garlic and ginger and cook until soft and golden, then add the turmeric, garam masala, tomato, chilli, mint, remaining salt and the lemon juice. Add the beans and stir well over medium heat for 5 minutes. Add 250 ml (8½ fl oz/1 cup) of the reserved cooking liquid, cover, and cook over low heat until the tomato and chilli are soft and the sauce has thickened. Serve with rice or Indian breads as part of a vegetarian meal.

Mattar Chilka Kari
Curried pea pods

Serves: 4

When green peas are young and tender, save the pods after shelling the peas – they are delicious when cooked this way.

pods from 500 g (1 lb 2 oz) peas

1 tablespoon ghee or oil

1 onion, finely chopped

1 teaspoon finely chopped fresh ginger

1 teaspoon ground turmeric

1 teaspoon salt

1 teaspoon garam masala (page 19)

½ teaspoon chilli powder (optional)

2 ripe tomatoes, diced

4 small potatoes, peeled and diced

Separate half of the pods. To do this, hold each half with the inner side towards you and bend the stalk end inwards so that the fleshy part of the pod cracks. Then pull downwards, peeling off and discarding the thin, silk-like inner lining of the pod. Wash the pods and remove any strings from the edges.

Heat the ghee in a frying pan over low heat. Add the onion and ginger and cook until soft and golden. Add the turmeric, salt, garam masala and chilli powder, if using, and stir-fry for 1–2 minutes, then add the tomato, potato and pea pods. Cover and cook until the potato and pea pods are tender – it may be necessary to add a few spoonfuls of water if the curry starts to stick to the base of the pan, but if it is cooked on low heat and stirred occasionally, the liquid from the tomato will be sufficient. This curry should be quite dry. Serve with Chapatis (page 23), Paratha (page 28) or rice.

Vegetables ✦

Dal

Lentil purée

Serves: 4–6

Any type of lentils can be used for this, but red lentils and mung dal are the quickest cooking types and do not need soaking. Other types of lentils should be soaked overnight before cooking.

250 g (9 oz/1 cup) red lentils

1½ tablespoons ghee or oil

1 large onion, thinly sliced

2 garlic cloves, finely chopped

1 teaspoon finely grated fresh ginger

½ teaspoon ground turmeric

1 teaspoon salt, or to taste

½ teaspoon garam masala (page 19)

Wash the lentils thoroughly, removing and discarding those that float on the surface. Drain well.

Heat the ghee in a saucepan over low heat. Add the onion, garlic and ginger and cook until the onion is golden brown. Add the turmeric and stir well to coat. Add the drained lentils and cook for 1–2 minutes, then add 750 ml (25½ fl oz/3 cups) hot water. Bring to the boil, then reduce the heat to low, cover, and simmer for 15–20 minutes, or until the lentils are just tender. Add the salt and garam masala, mix well and continue cooking until the lentils are soft and the consistency is similar to porridge – if there is too much liquid, leave the lid off the pan to speed up evaporation. Serve the dal plain or garnished with sliced onions, fried until deep golden brown. Eat with rice, Indian breads, or as a light meal by itself.

Alu Mattar Sukhe
Potato and pea dry curry

Serves: 6

500 g (1 lb 2 oz) potatoes

500 g (1 lb 2 oz) fresh peas in the pod

40 g (1½ oz) ghee

1 teaspoon panch phora (page 15)

1 large onion, finely chopped

2 tablespoons chopped fresh mint or
    coriander (cilantro) leaves

1 teaspoon finely grated fresh ginger

1 teaspoon ground turmeric

1½ teaspoons salt

½ teaspoon chilli powder (optional)

1 teaspoon garam masala (page 19)

1 tablespoon lemon juice

Peel and dice the potatoes. Shell the peas.

Heat the ghee in a saucepan over low heat. Add the panch phora and cook until the seeds start to brown, then add the onion and cook until it softens and starts to colour. Add the mint and ginger and cook for a few seconds, stirring well. Add the turmeric, salt and chilli powder, if using, to the pan and stir well. Add the potato and peas, and sprinkle over 60 ml (2 fl oz/¼ cup) hot water. Reduce the heat to low, cover, and cook for 20 minutes, shaking the pan occasionally. Sprinkle with the garam masala and lemon juice, cover again, and continue cooking for a further 10 minutes. Serve hot with rice or Chapatis (page 23).

Gobi Foogath
Spicy fried cabbage

Serves: 6

80 ml (2½ fl oz/⅓ cup) oil

1 large onion, thinly sliced

2–3 fresh green or red chillies, deseeded
and sliced

2 garlic cloves, finely chopped

1 teaspoon finely grated fresh ginger

1 teaspoon ground turmeric

½ head white cabbage, coarsely shredded

1½ teaspoons salt, or to taste

2 tablespoons desiccated (shredded) coconut

Heat the oil in a large saucepan over low heat. Add the onion and chilli and cook until the onion is soft. Add the garlic and ginger and stir-fry until golden. Add the turmeric and cabbage and stir-fry to combine, then cover and cook over low heat for 10–15 minutes or until the cabbage is tender. Sprinkle with the salt, add the coconut and stir well. Serve with rice and curries.

Gobi Bhaji
Spicy fried cauliflower

Serves: 4

2 tablespoons ghee or oil

1 teaspoon black mustard seeds

½ teaspoon panch phora (page 15)

1 large garlic clove, crushed

3 teaspoons finely grated fresh ginger

½ teaspoon ground turmeric

1 small head cauliflower, broken into florets

1 teaspoon salt

½ teaspoon garam masala (page 19)

Heat the oil in a saucepan over low heat. Add the mustard seeds and cook until they start to pop. Add the panch phora, garlic and ginger and stir-fry until golden. Add the turmeric, salt, cauliflower and 60 ml (2 fl oz/¼ cup) water and cook for 5 minutes, or until the cauliflower is tender. Sprinkle with the garam masala and serve with rice or Chapatis (page 23).

Palak Bhaji
Spicy fried spinach

Serves: 4–6

40 g (1½ oz) ghee

2 tablespoons oil

2 large onions, thinly sliced

2 garlic cloves, finely chopped

1 teaspoon finely grated fresh ginger

1 teaspoon cumin seeds

½ teaspoon black cumin seeds (optional)

½ teaspoon ground cumin

½ teaspoon ground coriander

½ teaspoon ground turmeric

¼ teaspoon chilli powder (optional)

1 teaspoon salt, or to taste

500 g (1 lb 2 oz) English spinach, stalks trimmed and rinsed well

Heat the ghee and oil in a large saucepan over low heat. Add the onion and cook until golden, then add the garlic and ginger and stir-fry for 1–2 minutes. Add the cumin seeds, black cumin seeds, if using, the ground cumin, coriander, turmeric, chilli powder, if using, and salt and mix well.

Add the spinach to the pan with only the water that remains on the leaves after washing. Toss to coat in the spicy mixture, then reduce the heat to low and cook, stirring frequently, until the spinach is tender – it may be necessary to add a little more water to prevent the spinach sticking to the pan. Serve with rice, Chapatis (page 23) or other Indian breads.

Alu Bartha (1)
Spicy mashed potatoes (cold)

Serves: 6

500 g (1 lb 2 oz) floury potatoes

40 g (1½ oz) ghee, melted

60 ml (2 fl oz/¼ cup) lemon juice

½ teaspoon salt, or to taste

125 ml (4 fl oz/½ cup) hot milk

25 g (1 oz/½ cup) finely chopped fresh mint leaves

2 spring onions (scallions) or 1 small onion, finely chopped

Cook the potatoes in their skins in a saucepan of boiling water until tender. Drain well, then peel and mash. Add the ghee, lemon juice and salt, and mix in just enough hot milk to give a smooth, creamy consistency. Stir through the mint and spring onion. To serve, pat the mashed potato into a flat shape on a plate, or pile in a bowl. Serve cold or at room temperature.

Alu Bartha (2)
Spicy mashed potatoes (hot)

Serves: 6

500 g (1 lb 2 oz) potatoes

1 tablespoon ghee or oil

½ teaspoon black mustard seeds

1 fresh green chilli, deseeded and sliced

1 small onion, finely chopped

½ teaspoon ground turmeric

1 teaspoon garam masala (page 19)

1 teaspoon salt

a pinch of chilli powder

1–2 tablespoons lemon juice

chopped fresh mint or coriander (cilantro) leaves to garnish

Cook the potatoes in their skins in a saucepan of boiling water until tender. Drain well, then peel and mash.

Heat the ghee in a saucepan over low heat. Add the mustard seeds and cook until they start to pop, then add the chilli and onion and cook until the onion is soft and golden. Add the turmeric, garam masala, salt and chilli powder and stir for a few moments, then add the lemon juice. Mix in the potatoes, stirring until well combined and heated through. Serve sprinkled with the mint or coriander leaves.

Gooda Bartha
Zucchini purée

Serves: 4

500 g (1 lb 2 oz) zucchini (courgette) or marrow (summer squash)

1 tablespoon ghee or oil

1 teaspoon cumin seeds

½ teaspoon black mustard seeds

2 fresh green chillies, deseeded and sliced

1 onion, finely chopped

½ teaspoon salt

½ teaspoon chilli powder (optional)

Peel and halve each zucchini lengthways. Scrape out and discard the seeds and roughly chop the flesh. Place the zucchini in a saucepan with enough water to cover and cook over low heat until soft. Drain well and mash.

Heat the ghee in a saucepan over low heat. Add the cumin and mustard seeds and stir-fry until the mustard seeds start to pop. Add the chilli and onion and cook until the onion softens. Add the zucchini, salt and chilli powder, if using, and cook for 5 minutes. Serve warm or at room temperature.

Sabzi Bhaji
Fried mixed vegetables

Serves: 6

This recipe is a colourful combination of lightly spiced vegetables – take care not to overcook them.

3 large carrots

250 g (9 oz) green beans

¼ head cauliflower

½ head small green cabbage

3 tablespoons ghee or oil

½ teaspoon black mustard seeds or
   panch phora (page 15)

8 curry leaves (optional)

2 garlic cloves, crushed

2 teaspoons finely grated fresh ginger

1 teaspoon ground turmeric

¼ teaspoon chilli powder or 1 fresh red
   chilli, deseeded and sliced

1½ teaspoons salt, or to taste

Peel the carrots and cut into thin matchsticks. Trim the beans, removing the strings if needed and slice diagonally. Cut the cauliflower into florets, leaving some stem on. Coarsely shred the cabbage.

Heat the ghee in a large frying pan over low heat. Add the mustard seeds and the curry leaves, if using, and cook for 2 minutes, stirring well. Add the garlic, ginger, turmeric and chilli and stir-fry for 1–2 minutes, then add the carrots, beans and cauliflower. Stir over medium heat until the vegetables are half-cooked, then add the cabbage and continue to stir-fry for a further 5 minutes, or until all the vegetables are tender but still crisp. Sprinkle with the salt, mix well, cover and cook for a final 2 minutes. Serve immediately.

Mattar Panir
Peas with fresh cheese

Serves: 4–6

Fresh homemade cheese is a favourite addition to vegetable curries, as it is an important source of protein for strict vegetarians. Make the panir as described on page 15. For convenience and speed, when panir is not commercially available, substitute baked ricotta. Frozen peas can be used instead of fresh.

250 g (9 oz) panir or baked ricotta cheese

125 ml (4 fl oz/½ cup) melted ghee or oil

2 onions, finely chopped

3 garlic cloves, finely chopped

2 teaspoons finely grated fresh ginger

2 teaspoons ground coriander

1 teaspoon ground cumin

1 teaspoon ground turmeric

1 teaspoon chilli powder (optional)

2 firm ripe tomatoes, chopped

1 teaspoon salt

1 teaspoon garam masala (page 19)

750 g (1 lb 11 oz) fresh or frozen peas

2 tablespoons finely chopped fresh mint or coriander (cilantro) leaves

If making the panir, let the curds hang in the muslin (cheesecloth) until cool, then squeeze out as much liquid as possible by twisting the muslin. Put the wrapped curds on a flat plate and put another plate or a chopping board on top. Weight it down and leave for about 6 hours until very firm. Remove the muslin and cut the cheese into small cubes. If not using immediately, cover with plastic wrap and refrigerate until needed. If using baked ricotta, cut into small cubes.

Heat the ghee or oil in a large frying pan and cook the cheese, in batches, turning them carefully so they brown on all sides. As each batch is done, remove to a plate with a slotted spoon.

Pour off all but 1 tablespoon of fat from the pan. Add the onion, garlic and ginger and cook over medium–low heat, stirring frequently, until the onion is golden. Add the ground spices and stir for 1 minute further, then add the tomatoes, salt and half of the garam masala. Cook and stir until the tomato is pulpy, adding a little hot water if the mixture seems too dry. Add the fresh peas, if using, and cook until they are just tender, about 20 minutes. Add the cheese and half of the mint, cover, and simmer for a further 10 minutes, or until the peas are cooked. Sprinkle with the remaining garam masala and mint and serve hot with rice or Chapatis (page 23).

Note

If using frozen peas, add at the same time as the cheese.

Alu Chap
Potato rissoles with peas

Serves: 4

1 kg (2 lb 6 oz) potatoes

salt to taste

20 g (¾ oz) ghee

1 onion, finely chopped

1 teaspoon finely grated fresh ginger

1 tablespoon chopped fresh coriander
(cilantro) leaves

½ teaspoon ground turmeric

½ teaspoon garam masala (page 19)

¼ teaspoon chilli powder, or to taste

1 teaspoon salt

310 g (11 oz/2 cups) fresh or frozen peas

oil for deep-frying

2 eggs, beaten

dry breadcrumbs for coating

Cook the potatoes in their skins in a saucepan of boiling water until tender. Drain well, then peel and mash until quite smooth, adding salt to taste.

Heat the ghee in a saucepan over low heat. Add the onion, ginger and coriander and cook until the onion is soft and golden. Add the turmeric, garam masala and chilli powder, if using, then stir in the salt and peas. Cover and cook until the peas are tender and all the liquid has been absorbed. If using fresh peas, add a little water when cooking them. Remove from the heat.

Divide the potato mixture into 8 even-sized portions and shape each one into a flat circle. Put a spoonful of the peas in the centre and enclose with the potato, moulding it smoothly into a patty shape.

Heat the oil in a large heavy-based saucepan over medium heat. Dip each rissole first in the egg, then roll in the breadcrumbs to coat on both sides. When the oil is hot, deep-fry the rissoles, 2 or 3 at a time, until golden brown all over. Drain on paper towel and serve hot.

Taazi Khumben Alu Mattar Kari
Curried mushrooms, potatoes and peas

Serves: 6

500 g (1 lb 2 oz) small button mushrooms

500 g (1 lb 2 oz) small new potatoes

1 tablespoon ghee or oil

1 small onion, thinly sliced

1 teaspoon finely grated fresh ginger

1 garlic clove, crushed (optional)

2 tablespoons finely chopped fresh
  coriander (cilantro) leaves

1 teaspoon ground turmeric

½ teaspoon chilli powder (optional)

155 g (5½ oz/1 cup) fresh or frozen peas

1½ teaspoons salt

1 teaspoon garam masala (page 19)

Wipe the mushrooms with damp paper towel. If the mushrooms are large, cut them in halves or quarters, leaving the stems on. Wash and scrub the potatoes and if large cut into halves or quarters.

Heat the ghee in a saucepan over medium heat. Add the onion and cook for 3 minutes, then add the ginger, garlic and coriander and stir-fry for 3–4 minutes. Add the turmeric and chilli powder, if using, stir together for 1 minute, then add the mushrooms, potato and peas. Add 125 ml (4 fl oz/½ cup) hot water and the salt and stir well. Cover, and cook over low heat for 15 minutes. Sprinkle with the garam masala and stir well, then re-cover and cook for a further 15 minutes, or until the potatoes are tender enough to be pierced with a skewer. Serve with rice or Indian bread.

Note

Frozen peas can be used instead of fresh, but add them during the last 15 minutes of cooking.

Dhingri Kari
Mushroom curry

Serves: 4

Choose large field mushrooms, because they have the strongest flavour.

500 g (1 lb 2 oz) mushrooms

2 leeks, white part only, or 4 spring onions (scallions)

2 tablespoons ghee or oil

2 garlic cloves, crushed

½ teaspoon finely grated fresh ginger

6 curry leaves

2 teaspoons curry powder

1 teaspoon salt

½ teaspoon garam masala (page 19)

125 ml (4 fl oz/½ cup) thick coconut milk (pages 6–8)

2 teaspoons lemon juice

Wipe the mushrooms clean, remove the stems and chop the caps into quarters. Thinly slice the leeks or spring onions.

Heat the ghee in a saucepan over medium heat. Add the garlic, ginger, curry leaves and leek and cook until soft but not brown. Add the curry powder, salt and mushrooms and continue to stir over low heat until the mushrooms are soft. Cover and cook for 8–10 minutes. Sprinkle with the garam masala, add the coconut milk and cook uncovered, stirring constantly, until just heated through. Remove from the heat and stir in the lemon juice. Serve with rice or vegetable pilaus.

Gujarati Khattai Alu
Gujarati potatoes

Serves: 4–6

500 g (1 lb 2 oz) floury potatoes, peeled and diced

1 tablespoon tamarind pulp

2 teaspoons brown sugar

1½ tablespoons ghee or oil

½ teaspoon black mustard seeds

½ teaspoon ground turmeric

½ teaspoon chilli powder

1 teaspoon ground coriander

1 teaspoon ground cumin

1 teaspoon salt, or to taste

2 fresh green chillies, deseeded and sliced

2 tablespoons desiccated (shredded) coconut

Soak the tamarind pulp in 60 ml (2 fl oz/¼ cup) hot water for 10 minutes. Squeeze to dissolve the pulp in the water, then strain, discarding the seeds and fibre. Dissolve the sugar in the tamarind liquid.

Heat the ghee in a saucepan over low heat and cook the mustard seeds until they start to pop. Add the turmeric, chilli powder, coriander and cumin and cook over low heat for 1 minute. Add the potato and toss gently to coat in the seasoning. Add the salt and 60 ml (2 fl oz/¼ cup) hot water, cover, and cook over low heat for 15 minutes. Add the tamarind liquid, chilli and desiccated coconut and stir well. Cover and cook for a further 5–10 minutes, or until the potato is cooked through. Serve hot with rice or Chapatis (page 23).

Alu Bhaji
Savoury fried potatoes

Serves: 4

Serve these as an accompaniment to Thosai (page 52) or any of the Indian breads. You can also mash this potato mixture slightly and use it to fill Chapatis (page 23), Puris (page 26) and Kachoris (page 26) before cooking.

500 g (1 lb 2 oz) potatoes

1 tablespoon ghee or oil

¼ teaspoon black mustard seeds

2 onions, finely chopped

½ teaspoon ground turmeric

1 teaspoon chilli powder, or to taste

1 teaspoon salt

Cook the potatoes in their skins in a saucepan of boiling water until tender. Drain well, then peel and dice.

Heat the ghee in a saucepan over low heat. Add the mustard seeds and cook until they start to pop. Add the onion and cook until it is soft and golden. Add the turmeric and chilli powder and stir, then add the potato, sprinkle over the salt and toss gently to coat in the seasonings. Serve hot or cold.

Baigan Dahi
Eggplant with yoghurt

Serves: 6

2 eggplants (aubergines)

1 tablespoon ghee or oil

2 onions, finely chopped

3 garlic cloves, finely chopped

2 teaspoons finely grated fresh ginger

2 teaspoons ground coriander

1 teaspoon ground cumin

½ teaspoon ground turmeric

½ teaspoon chilli powder

1½ teaspoons salt, or to taste

½ teaspoon garam masala (page 19)
  (optional)

2 teaspoons sugar (optional)

250 g (9 oz/1 cup) plain yoghurt

Put the eggplants under a preheated grill (broiler), about 15 cm (6 in) from the heat and grill (broil) until the skins blacken and the eggplants are completely soft. Cool, then peel the skin and roughly mash or finely chop the flesh.

Heat the ghee in a saucepan over low heat. Add the onion, garlic and ginger and cook until the onion is soft and golden. Add the coriander, cumin, turmeric and chilli powder and stir-fry for 1 minute. Add the salt and eggplant, stirring to combine, and cook for 3–4 minutes. Sprinkle with the garam masala, if using, cover, and cook for a further 5 minutes. Season with more salt if necessary, and, if liked, a little sugar. Mash the yoghurt until smooth and mix into the eggplant before serving. Serve with rice, curries and other accompaniments.

Brinjal Bartha
Eggplant purée

Serves: 6

3 tablespoons ghee or oil

2 onions, finely chopped

1½ teaspoons finely grated fresh ginger

½ teaspoon ground turmeric

½ teaspoon chilli powder

2 teaspoons salt

1 teaspoon garam masala (page 19)

2 large eggplants (aubergines), diced

2 large ripe tomatoes, diced

Heat the ghee in a saucepan over medium heat. Add the onion and ginger and stir-fry until they start to brown. Add the turmeric, chilli powder, salt and garam masala and mix well. Add the eggplant and tomato and stir well to combine. Reduce the heat to low, cover, and cook until the vegetables have softened and the purée has thickened, stirring often to prevent them from sticking to the base of the pan. Remove from the heat and serve hot or cold.

Piaz Bhaji
Spicy fried onions or leeks

Serves: 4–6

5–6 large leeks, white part only, or
    3 large onions, peeled

2 tablespoons ghee or oil

1 teaspoon panch phora (page 15) or
    cumin seeds

1 teaspoon ground turmeric

1 teaspoon finely grated fresh ginger

1 teaspoon garam masala (page 19)

1 teaspoon salt, or to taste

Wash the leeks well, if using. Thickly slice the leeks or onions.

Heat the ghee in a large saucepan over low heat. Add the panch phora and stir-fry for 1–2 minutes, then add the turmeric and ginger and stir-fry for 1 minute. Add the leek or onion and continue stir-frying for 5 minutes. Sprinkle the garam masala and salt into the pan, cover, and cook until tender. Serve hot.

Bhendi Bhaji
Spicy fried okra

Serves: 4–6

It is important to buy tender okra, for the mature beans are tough and stringy. Test by bending the tip of the bean – if tender, it will snap, but if it is old it will merely bend and you will not be able to break it.

500 g (1 lb 2 oz) okra
2 tablespoons ghee or oil
½ teaspoon panch phora (page 15)
1 onion, finely chopped
½ teaspoon ground turmeric
½ teaspoon salt, or to taste
½ teaspoon garam masala (page 19)
½ teaspoon chilli powder (optional)

Wash the okra, cut off the stems and cut into bite-sized pieces.

Heat the ghee in a frying pan over low heat. Add the panch phora and cook for 1 minute, then add the onion and stir-fry until it starts to turn golden. Add the turmeric, salt, garam masala and chilli powder, if using. Add the okra, stir well, then cover and cook, stirring occasionally, until the okra is tender. Serve with rice or Chapatis (page 23).

Bhendi Kari
Okra curry

Serves: 4–6

500 g (1 lb 2 oz) okra

1 tablespoon ghee or oil

1 large onion, thinly sliced

2 fresh green chillies, halved lengthways
and deseeded

1 garlic clove, thinly sliced

½ teaspoon finely grated fresh ginger

½ teaspoon ground turmeric

½ teaspoon ground coriander

½ teaspoon ground cumin

375 ml (12½ fl oz/1½ cups) thin coconut
milk (pages 6–8) or buttermilk

salt to taste

Wash the okra, cut off the stems and cut into bite-sized pieces.

Heat the ghee in a frying pan over medium–low heat.
Add the onion and chilli and stir-fry until the onion is
golden. Add the garlic, ginger and turmeric and stir-fry
for 1 minute further, then add the okra and cook for
3–4 minutes. Add the coriander, cumin and coconut milk
and season with salt, to taste. Continue to simmer over low
heat for 10–12 minutes, or until the okra is tender. Serve
hot with rice.

Accompaniments

✦

Khira Pachchadi
Cucumbers in spiced yoghurt

Serves: 4–6

25 g (1 oz/¼ cup) desiccated (shredded) coconut

2 long (telegraph) cucumbers, peeled, deseeded and grated

2 fresh green chillies, deseeded and chopped

1 teaspoon salt

375 g (13 oz/1½ cups) plain yoghurt

1 teaspoon ghee or oil

1 teaspoon black mustard seeds

½ teaspoon nigella seeds (optional)

Sprinkle 60 ml (2 fl oz/¼ cup) hot water over the coconut in a bowl and toss lightly to moisten. Add the cucumber, chilli, salt and yoghurt and stir well.

Heat the ghee in a small frying pan over low heat. Add the mustard seeds and nigella seeds and cook until they start to pop. Stir into the yoghurt mixture. Serve cold.

Kela Pachchadi
Bananas in spiced yoghurt

Serves: 6

3 tablespoons freshly grated or desiccated (shredded) coconut

250 g (9 oz/1 cup) yoghurt

2 tablespoons lemon juice

2 teaspoons sugar

½ teaspoon salt

⅛ teaspoon chilli powder, or to taste

3 large ripe bananas, peeled and sliced

1 teaspoon ghee or oil

1 teaspoon cumin seeds

1 teaspoon black mustard seeds

If using desiccated coconut, sprinkle 1 tablespoon hot water over it to moisten. Season the yoghurt with lemon juice, sugar, salt and chilli powder, and stir in the banana and coconut.

Heat the ghee in a small saucepan over low heat. Add the cumin seeds and mustard seeds and cook until they start to pop. Stir into the yoghurt mixture. Serve with a curry meal.

Baigan Pachchadi
Spiced eggplant with yoghurt

Serves: 4–6

1 tablespoon oil

1 teaspoon black mustard seeds

1 onion, finely chopped

2 fresh green chillies, deseeded and sliced

1 eggplant (aubergine), peeled and diced

1 small ripe tomato, diced

1 teaspoon salt

1 teaspoon garam masala (page 19)

½ teaspoon chilli powder (optional)

250 g (9 oz/1 cup) plain yoghurt

2 tablespoons chopped fresh coriander
(cilantro) leaves

Heat the oil in a frying pan over low heat. Add the mustard seeds and cook until they start to pop. Add the onion and chilli and stir-fry until the onion is soft.

Add the eggplant to the pan and stir-fry for 3 minutes, then add the tomato, salt, garam masala and chilli powder, if using, and stir to combine. Add 60 ml (2 fl oz/¼ cup) water, cover, and simmer until the eggplant and tomato can be mashed to a purée. Cool, stir in the yoghurt and half of the coriander. Serve hot, garnished with the remaining coriander.

Palak Raita

Spinach with yoghurt and spices

Serves: 4–6

....

500 g (1 lb 2 oz) English spinach leaves

1 tablespoon ghee or oil

1 teaspoon black mustard seeds

1 teaspoon cumin seeds

1 teaspoon ground cumin

½ teaspoon fenugreek seeds

½ teaspoon salt, or to taste

a pinch of chilli powder or cayenne pepper
   (optional)

250 g (9 oz/1 cup) plain yoghurt

Wash the spinach leaves and remove any tough stems. Tear the leaves into pieces and place into a large saucepan with the moisture on the leaves or add 1 tablespoon water. Cover and steam over low heat until the spinach has wilted. Drain and chop finely.

Heat the ghee in a small saucepan over low heat. Add the mustard seeds and cook until they start to pop. Add the cumin seeds, ground cumin and fenugreek seeds and stir-fry with a wooden spoon until the fenugreek seeds are golden brown – be careful they do not burn. Remove from the heat, stir in the salt and chilli powder, if using, and allow to cool. Mix in the yoghurt, then stir this mixture into the spinach. Serve cold or at room temperature as an accompaniment to a meal.

Piaz Sambal
Onion sambal

Serves: 4–6

2 tablespoons lemon juice

2 red onions, thinly sliced

½ teaspoon chilli powder, or to taste

½ teaspoon salt

Sprinkle the lemon juice over the onion in a bowl and stir through the chilli powder and salt until well combined. Serve as an accompaniment to a meal of rice and curries, or with Lamb kebabs (page 115) and Paratha (page 28).

Khira Raita
Cucumber with yoghurt

Serves: 6

2 long (telegraph) cucumbers

2 teaspoons salt

1 small garlic clove, crushed

¼ teaspoon finely grated fresh ginger

250 g (9 oz/1 cup) plain yoghurt

lemon juice to taste

Peel and thinly slice the cucumbers. Place in a bowl, sprinkle over the salt and refrigerate for about 1 hour. Pour off any liquid, pressing out as much as possible.

Mix the garlic and ginger into the yoghurt, then stir in the cucumber and combine well. Taste and add more salt or lemon juice, as desired. Serve chilled.

Variation

For a richer version of cucumber raita, substitute 250 g (9 oz/1 cup) sour cream for the yoghurt, or 125 g (4½ oz/½ cup) thick (double/heavy) cream mixed with the same amount of plain yoghurt.

Piaz Ka Dhania Pattar Salat
Onion and coriander leaf salad

Serves: 4–6

2 onions, thinly sliced

salt to taste

2 tablespoons lemon juice

1 tablespoon (or more) chopped fresh
coriander (cilantro) leaves

Combine all the ingredients in a bowl. Cover with plastic wrap and refrigerate until ready to serve.

Tamatar Salat
Tomato salad with mint and spring onions

Serves: 4–6

4 firm red tomatoes

6 spring onions (scallions)

10 g (¼ oz/½ cup) fresh mint leaves

60 ml (2 fl oz/¼ cup) lemon juice

½ teaspoon salt, or to taste

2 teaspoons sugar

½ teaspoon chilli powder (optional)

Peel the tomatoes and cut into thin wedges. Thinly slice the spring onions and chop the mint leaves. Mix the lemon juice, salt, sugar and chilli powder, if using, together. Stir until the sugar dissolves, then pour over the combined ingredients and mix lightly but thoroughly. Cover and chill until serving time.

Kachumbar
Parsi-style onion salad

Serves: 4–6

This relish can be hot or not so hot. If you want the milder version, the chillies should be deseeded (see handling of chillies, page 8). If deseeded chillies are still likely to be too hot for your taste, substitute about 80 g (2¾ oz/½ cup) thinly sliced red or green capsicum (bell pepper).

2 onions, thinly sliced

salt for sprinkling

2 tablespoons tamarind pulp

2 tablespoons grated palm sugar (jaggery)

2 firm ripe tomatoes, diced

1 tablespoon finely grated fresh ginger

3 fresh red or green chillies, sliced

2 tablespoons chopped fresh coriander
  (cilantro) leaves

Sprinkle the onion generously with the salt and set aside for 1 hour. Press out as much liquid as possible and rinse in cold water. Drain well.

Soak the tamarind pulp in 60 ml (2 fl oz/¼ cup) hot water for 10 minutes. Squeeze to dissolve the pulp in the water, then strain, discarding the seeds and fibres. Put the palm sugar in the tamarind liquid and stir to dissolve.

Mix together the onion, sweetened tamarind liquid, tomato, ginger, chilli and coriander. Cover with plastic wrap and refrigerate until ready to serve. Serve chilled.

Am Ka Achar
Green mango pickle

My husband, Reuben, was positively inspired when it came to making pickles. All the pickle recipes that follow come from his recipe file – which probably would not exist had I not given it to him inscribed, 'To the best cook in the world from his assistant and typist'; a cunning ploy to make him record his recipes. But half the time I would follow him around the kitchen, noting his every move and writing busily between complying with his demands for spices, vinegar, salt and just about everything else he needed. Oh well, genius must be pandered to, I suppose. The mangoes for this pickle should be so unripe that it is possible to cut through the stone and kernel without too much effort.

12 green mangoes

50 red or green chillies

3 teaspoons salt

2 teaspoons fenugreek seeds

625 ml (21 fl oz/2½ cups) malt vinegar

10 large garlic cloves

100 g (3½ oz/½ cup) chopped fresh ginger

50 g (1¾ oz/½ cup) ground cumin

50 g (1¾ oz/½ cup) ground coriander

1.25 litres (42 fl oz/5 cups) mustard oil, plus extra for bottling

2 tablespoons black mustard seeds

2 tablespoons curry leaves

1½ tablespoons fennel seeds

1½ tablespoons nigella seeds

1 tablespoon ground turmeric

1 tablespoon chilli powder, or to taste

2½ tablespoons salt, or to taste

Wash the mangoes well and cut each through the stone into 8 sections. Split the chillies in half lengthways almost up to the stem end. Sprinkle the mango and chillies with salt and dry for 3 days in the sun.

Soak the fenugreek seeds in a bowl overnight in just enough of the malt vinegar to cover.

Put the soaked fenugreek seeds, garlic, ginger, cumin and coriander into a food processor with enough vinegar to facilitate blending and process to make a smooth purée.

Heat the mustard oil in a large stainless steel or enamel saucepan until hot, then add the mustard seeds, curry leaves, fennel seeds, nigella seeds, turmeric and chilli powder and mix well. Return to medium heat and stir constantly with a wooden spoon for 2 minutes. Add the salted mango, chillies and remaining vinegar. Bring to the boil, then reduce the heat to low and simmer for 30 minutes, or until the oil rises to the surface and the spices become aromatic. Add the salt to taste, remove from the heat and allow to cool.

Pour the pickle into sterilised airtight jars and top each jar with a little extra oil. Always use a dry spoon when taking pickle from the jar and it should keep for years.

Note

Strips of salted, dried mango are available in some Asian grocery stores. Substitute 500 g (1 lb 2 oz) salted dried mango for the fresh mangoes in this recipe and omit the salting and drying process.

Accompaniments ✦

Nimboo Ka Achar
Lime or lemon oil pickle

Proceed as for mango oil pickle (page 163), but use 12–15 lemons (instead of the mangoes) that have been quartered, salted and dried in the sun for 3 days.

Ananas Achar
Pineapple oil pickle

This pickle is based on the spice combination for mango pickle (page 163). Instead of using mangoes, use 2 large pineapples that are ripe, but not in any way overripe. Remove the skin of each pineapple and remove the 'eyes', then cut into wedges lengthways and remove the hard core. Chop the flesh and squeeze out as much juice as possible. Proceed with the recipe, adding 110 g (4 oz/½ cup) sugar at the simmering stage if a slightly sweeter pickle is desired. Continue to cook until the oil separates and rises to the surface. Cool, bottle and seal.

Jhinga Achar
Dried prawn pickle

This is a particularly delicious and popular Indian pickle which keeps well. Follow the recipe for mango pickle (page 163), substituting 1 kg (2 lb 3 oz) dried shrimp or dried small prawns for the mangoes. If using prawns, soak them in a mild vinegar for 2 hours, then drain the vinegar and proceed to cook the recipe following the directions on page 163. If possible, use bird's eye chillies, which are very hot. It is not necessary to split or salt them. Increase the cooking time to 45 minutes.

Tamatar Kasaundi
Tomato oil pickle

If you grow your own tomatoes, this is an excellent way to make use of a bountiful harvest.

1½ tablespoons black mustard seeds

375 ml (12½ fl oz/1½ cups) malt vinegar

150 g (5½ oz/¾ cup) chopped fresh ginger

20 garlic cloves, chopped

310 ml (10½ fl oz/1¼ cups) oil

1½ tablespoons ground turmeric

75 g (2¾ oz/¾ cup) ground cumin

1–2 tablespoons chilli powder, or to taste

2 kg (4 lb 6 oz) firm ripe tomatoes, peeled and chopped

20 fresh green chillies, halved lengthways and deseeded

220 g (8 oz/1 cup) sugar

1 tablespoon salt

Soak the mustard seeds overnight in the vinegar. Transfer to a food processor and process to a paste. Add the ginger and garlic and process to make a smooth purée.

Heat the oil in a large heavy-based saucepan over low heat. Add the turmeric, cumin and chilli powder and cook for 3–4 minutes, stirring well. Add the tomato, chilli, vinegar purée, sugar and salt. Simmer until the tomato is reduced to a pulp and the oil starts to rise to the surface. Taste and add more salt if required. Remove from the heat and allow to cool. Bottle and seal when cold.

Pour the kasaundi into sterilised airtight jars and top each jar with a little extra oil. Leave to mature for 1 week before using. Once opened, the kasaundi can be stored in the refrigerator for up to 3 months.

Imli Chatni
Tamarind chutney

Makes: 280 g (10 oz/1 cup)

3 tablespoons dried tamarind pulp

1 teaspoon salt

2 teaspoons soft brown sugar

1 teaspoon ground cumin

½ teaspoon ground fennel

2 teaspoons finely grated fresh ginger

lemon juice to taste

a pinch of chilli powder (optional)

Soak the tamarind pulp in 250 ml (8½ fl oz/1 cup) hot water for 10 minutes. Squeeze to dissolve the pulp in the water, then strain, discarding the seeds and fibres.

Add the remaining ingredients to the tamarind liquid and stir to mix well. Taste and adjust the seasoning with salt, lemon juice or chilli powder, if needed. Store in an airtight jar in the refrigerator for up to 2 days. Serve with Pani puri (page 54).

Podina Chatni
Mint chutney

Makes: 560 g (1 lb 4 oz/2 cups)

20 g (¾ oz/1 cup) firmly packed fresh mint leaves

6 spring onions (scallions), chopped

2 fresh green chillies, deseeded and chopped

1 garlic clove (optional)

1 teaspoon salt

2 teaspoons sugar

1 teaspoon garam masala (page 19)

80 ml (2½ fl oz/⅓ cup) lemon juice

Put all the ingredients in a food processor and process to make a smooth paste. Alternatively, finely chop the mint, spring onions and chillies and pound using a mortar and pestle until ground to a paste. Mix in the remaining ingredients and 2 tablespoons water. Cover and refrigerate until ready to serve. Store in an airtight jar in the refrigerator for up to 3 days.

Dhania Chatni

Fresh coriander chutney

Makes: 2 cups

20 g (¾ oz/1 cup) firmly packed fresh
  coriander (cilantro) leaves

6 spring onions (scallions), chopped

2 fresh green chillies, deseeded and chopped

1 garlic clove (optional)

1 teaspoon salt

2 teaspoons sugar

1 teaspoon garam masala (page 19)

80 ml (2½ fl oz/⅓ cup) lemon juice

1 teaspoon finely grated fresh ginger
  (optional)

Put all the ingredients in a food processor and process to make a smooth paste. Alternatively, finely chop the coriander, spring onions and chillies and pound using a mortar and pestle. Mix in the remaining ingredients and 2 tablespoons water. Cover and refrigerate until ready to serve. Store in an airtight jar in the refrigerator for up to 3 days.

Nariyal Chatni

Green coconut chutney

Serves: 6

Traditionally, this chutney is served as an accompaniment to Thosai (page 52), but it is equally acceptable as an accompaniment to any other kind of Indian meal.

1 lemon

1–2 fresh green chillies, deseeded and chopped

10 g (¼ oz/½ cup) fresh mint or coriander (cilantro) leaves, or a combination of both

2 spring onions (scallions), roughly chopped

1 teaspoon salt

90 g (3 oz/1 cup) desiccated (shredded) coconut

1 teaspoon ghee or oil

2 teaspoons black mustard seeds

2 teaspoons cumin seeds

Peel the lemon so that no white pith remains. Cut the flesh into pieces and remove the seeds. Put the lemon into a food processor or blender with the chilli, mint or coriander leaves, spring onion and salt and process to make a purée. Add the coconut and continue processing to make a smooth paste, scraping down the sides as you go and adding a little more liquid if necessary.

Heat the ghee in a small frying pan over low heat. Add the mustard seeds and cumin seeds and cook until they start to pop. Add to the coconut mixture and stir well to combine. Store in an airtight jar in the refrigerator for up to 3 days.

Am Chatni
Sweet mango chutney

Serves: 6

This is not one of the fresh chutneys, which are the genuine chutneys of India. It is more like a thick jam, which, though not originally Indian, has come to be extremely popular and goes very well with Indian food.

8–10 large unripe mangoes, peeled, stones removed and chopped

3 teaspoons salt

8 large dried red chillies, stems removed

750 ml (25½ fl oz/3 cups) malt vinegar

5 garlic cloves

100 g (3½ oz/½ cup) chopped fresh ginger

1 teaspoon garam masala (page 19)

495 g (1 lb 2 oz/2¼ cups) sugar

125 g (4½ oz/1 cup) sultanas (golden raisins)

Put the mango in a large bowl and sprinkle with the salt. Soak the dried chillies in a little of the vinegar for 10 minutes.

Put the chillies and vinegar into a food processor with the garlic and ginger and process to combine – it does not matter if pieces of chilli remain. Alternatively, you can pound the soaked chillies using a mortar and pestle and finely grate the garlic and ginger, then stir well to combine.

Put the remaining vinegar into a large stainless steel saucepan with the chilli paste, garam masala and sugar and bring to the boil. Reduce the heat to low and simmer for 15 minutes. Add the mango and sultanas and continue to simmer until thick and syrupy. Remove from the heat and allow to cool. Pour into sterilised airtight jars. The sweet mango chutney can be stored without refrigeration for many months.

Note

1.5 kg (3 lb 5 oz) green apples, apricots or other suitable fruit may be used in place of mangoes.

Desserts

✦

Rabri
Condensed milk dessert

Serves: 4

This condensed milk doesn't come from a tin – it is made by boiling down pure fresh milk until most of the water content has evaporated. It may sound like a lot of trouble, but the end result is so vastly different from any short-cut method that it is worth trying at least once.

1.5 litres (51 fl oz/6 cups) milk

80 g (2¾ oz/⅓ cup) caster (superfine) sugar

2 drops kewra essence (glossary) or
  2 tablespoons rosewater

1 tablespoon slivered blanched almonds

1 tablespoon slivered blanched
  pistachio nuts

Put the milk into a heavy-based saucepan and bring to the boil, stirring constantly. Keep it cooking steadily and continue stirring until it is reduced to about 500 ml (17 fl oz/2 cups) and is thick. Reduce the heat, add the sugar and stir until the sugar has dissolved. Remove from the heat and stir well, scraping in particles of dried milk from the side of the pan and mixing them in. Allow to cool slightly, then add the flavouring when it is lukewarm. Pour into a serving bowl and sprinkle over the nuts. Refrigerate before serving.

Note

Use raw unsalted pistachio nuts and boil them for 1 minute to bring out their green colour and make it easy to slip off their skins.

Kheer
Rice pudding

Serves: 4–6

95 g (3¼ oz/½ cup) short-grain rice

2 litres (68 fl oz/8 cups) milk

4 cardamom pods

275 g (9½ oz/1¼ cups) sugar

2 tablespoons slivered blanched almonds (optional)

¼ teaspoon ground cardamom

¼ teaspoon freshly grated nutmeg

1 tablespoon rosewater

freshly grated nutmeg to serve

Wash the rice and boil for 5 minutes in water. Drain well.

Put the milk and cardamom pods into a large saucepan over medium–high heat and bring to the boil. Add the rice, reduce the heat to low, and simmer, stirring occasionally, for 1 hour, or until the rice is very soft and the milk quite thick. As the milk thickens it will be necessary to stir frequently with a wooden spoon, scraping the milk from the base of the pan. Add the sugar and almonds, if using, to the pan and continue cooking until the consistency is like that of porridge. Remove from the heat; discard the cardamom pods. If you think the flavour needs intensifying, add some ground cardamom and nutmeg. Allow to cool a little, then stir in the rosewater. Spoon the rice pudding into a large bowl or in individual portions, garnished with a little nutmeg. Serve warm or chilled.

Shrikhand
Saffron yoghurt dessert

Serves: 4–6

An exotic dessert, easy to prepare and a perfect conclusion to a spicy Indian meal. Also known in Northern India, where the dish originated, as Honeymoon Sweet.

500 g (1 lb 2 oz/2 cups) Greek-style yoghurt

115 g (4 oz/½ cup) caster (superfine) sugar, or to taste

1 tablespoon rosewater

¼ teaspoon ground cardamom

¼ teaspoon saffron strands

1 tablespoon boiling water

2 tablespoons pistachio kernels

In a bowl, whisk together the yoghurt, sugar, rosewater and cardamom until well combined and the sugar has dissolved.

In a small dry frying pan, lightly toast the saffron strands to remove any moisture, then remove from the pan and crush in a cup with the back of a teaspoon to make a fine powder. Add the boiling water and stir to combine, then add to the yoghurt mixture, stirring well. If using ground saffron, omit the toasting and crushing step.

Blanch the pistachio kernels in a saucepan of boiling water for 30 seconds then drain well. Allow to cool slightly, rub off the skins and chop finely. Sprinkle over the top of the shrikhand and serve.

Soojee Halwa
Semolina pudding

Serves: 6

170 g (6 oz/¾ cup) sugar

60 ml (2 fl oz/¼ cup) milk

¼ teaspoon powdered Spanish saffron

125 g (4½ oz) ghee

90 g (3 oz/¾ cup) fine semolina

2 tablespoons sultanas (golden raisins)

2 tablespoons slivered almonds, plus extra to garnish

1 teaspoon ground cardamom

Lightly butter a 1 litre (34 fl oz/4 cup) capacity serving dish.

Put the sugar, milk, saffron and 310 ml (10½ fl oz/1¼ cups) water into a saucepan and bring to the boil, stirring to dissolve the sugar. Remove from the heat and set aside.

Melt the ghee in a separate saucepan over low heat. Add the semolina and cook until the mixture turns golden, stirring constantly. Add the sugar syrup, sultanas, almonds and cardamom and cook over medium heat, stirring with a wooden spoon, until the mixture thickens and leaves the side of the pan. Remove from the heat. Pour the pudding mixture into the prepared dish and allow to cool.

When the pudding is cold, cut into diamond shapes and decorate with the extra almonds. This halwa can be served warm or cold, with or without cream. A popular way of serving it in India is with Puris (deep-fried Indian bread, page 26) and, surprising though it may seem to Westerners, at the beginning of a meal instead of at the end.

Gajjar Kheer
Carrot pudding

Serves: 4

1 litre (34 fl oz/4 cups) milk

⅛ teaspoon saffron strands

250 g (9 oz) carrots, peeled and grated

110 g (4 oz/½ cup) sugar

2 tablespoons ground almonds (optional)

⅛ teaspoon ground cardamom

Put the milk into a large heavy-based saucepan and bring to the boil. Remove 2 tablespoons of the boiling milk and soak the saffron strands in it.

Add the carrot to the boiling milk, reduce the heat to low and simmer for about 30 minutes, or until the carrots are soft and the mixture has thickened. Add the sugar, almonds, if using, cardamom and saffron mixture and stir until the sugar dissolves, then continue to simmer, stirring occasionally until the mixture is the consistency of a creamy rice pudding. Spoon into serving bowls and serve warm or cold.

Perhas
Milk sweetmeat

Makes: 10–12 pieces

....

1.25 litres (42 fl oz/5 cups) milk

1 teaspoon ghee

115 g (4 oz/½ cup) caster (superfine) sugar

¼ teaspoon ground cardamom or freshly
  grated nutmeg

slivered almonds or pistachio nuts
  (optional)

Put the milk into a large heavy-based saucepan and bring to the boil, stirring constantly, until the milk thickens and resembles the consistency of uncooked pastry. Remove from the heat, allow to cool, then crumble into small pieces.

Heat the ghee in a small saucepan over low heat. Add the crumbled milk mixture and stir over low heat until heated through. Add the sugar and stir constantly with a wooden spoon until the sugar has dissolved and the mixture is hot. Remove from the heat and add the cardamom, beating with a whisk until the mixture is smooth.

Allow to cool slightly, then roll into small balls, place in a serving dish and flatten slightly into a disc shape. The discs will not get hard but will have a soft fudge-like texture. Decorate each disc with a few slices of almond or pistachio nut, if desired.

Mysore Pak
Besan sweetmeat

Makes: 12–15 pieces

....

140 g (5 oz/⅔ cup) sugar

60 g (2 oz) besan (chickpea flour), sifted

185 g (6½ oz) ghee

½ teaspoon natural almond extract

½ teaspoon ground cardamom

Put the sugar and 60 ml (2 fl oz/¼ cup) water into a saucepan over low heat and stir until the sugar has dissolved. Bring to the boil for 5 minutes, then remove from the heat and set aside.

Heat two-thirds of the ghee in a heavy-based saucepan over low heat. Add the besan gradually and cook, stirring often, for about 5 minutes. Add the sugar syrup and continue cooking for a further 5 minutes, stirring constantly. Add the remaining ghee gradually (this can be melted and poured in or, if softened to room temperature, added by spoonfuls) and cook for 7–10 minutes, stirring constantly and making sure it doesn't brown. Pour into a lightly greased serving dish and cut into about 12 or 15 diamond shapes before it hardens.

Barfi Badam
Almond cream sweetmeat

Makes: about 16 pieces

....

1 litre (34 fl oz/4 cups) milk

165 g (6 oz/¾ cup) sugar

125 g (4½ oz/1¼ cups) ground almonds

a pinch of ground cardamom

2 tablespoons blanched pistachio nuts, halved

edible silver leaf (optional)

Put the milk in a heavy-based saucepan and bring to the boil, stirring constantly, until the milk has reduced and is very thick. Add the sugar, reduce the heat to low and simmer for 10 minutes. Add the ground almonds and continue to cook and stir until the mixture comes away from the side of the pan.

Remove from the heat, sprinkle over the cardamom and mix well. Pour into a lightly buttered serving dish, smooth the top with the back of a buttered spoon and cool slightly. Use a knife to score about 16 diamond shapes in the sweetmeat and decorate with the pistachios and silver leaf, if desired.

Before it is quite firm, cut with a sharp knife along the markings, then leave to get cold before separating into pieces.

Barfi Pista
Pistachio cream sweetmeat

Makes: about 16 pieces

....

To make a pistachio cream sweetmeat, follow the method for Barfi badam (above), substituting 100 g (3½ oz/⅔ cup) pistachio kernels for the ground almonds. Blanch the pistachio kernels in boiling water for 2 minutes, then remove the skins and pound to a paste using a mortar and pestle.

Kela Halwa
Banana sweetmeat

Makes: about 24 pieces

2½ tablespoons ghee

5 large ripe bananas, peeled and chopped

165 g (6 oz/¾ cup) sugar

2 tablespoons rosewater

½ teaspoon ground cardamom

Note

*Because this makes only a small quantity,
I use an oblong dish 20 × 8 cm (8 × 3¼ in)
to get the correct thickness of halwa.*

Heat the ghee in a large heavy-based frying pan. Add the banana and cook for 5 minutes, or until soft, stirring frequently so they do not brown. Remove from the heat and mash the banana in the pan.

Add 60 ml (2 fl oz/¼ cup) water to the banana and continue to cook over low heat for 3 minutes, stirring constantly. Add the sugar and another 250 ml (8½ fl oz/1 cup) water and stir constantly over medium heat until the sugar melts, then continue cooking and stirring for 15–20 minutes, or until the mixture is quite thick.

Remove from the heat and sprinkle in the rosewater and cardamom, stirring well to combine. Pour into a lightly buttered serving dish. If any ghee separates from the mixture, pour it off. When the halwa is cool, cut into small squares. This halwa can also be served warm.

Jalebi
Deep-fried batter sweetmeat

Makes: about 25

Jalebis are coils of crisply fried batter about the size of a saucer with a rose-scented syrup inside the coil. How the syrup gets inside is a mystery unless you do some research on the subject. In the bazaars and sweet shops, pyramids of brilliant orange jalebis up to a metre (three feet) high testify to the popularity of this sweet, and are quickly demolished.

Batter

300 g (10½ oz/2 cups) plain (all-purpose) flour, sifted

90 g (3 oz/½ cup) rice flour, sifted

7 g (¼ oz) fresh compressed yeast or scant ½ teaspoon dried yeast

¼ teaspoon saffron strands

2 tablespoons boiling water

1 tablespoon plain yoghurt

oil for deep-frying

Syrup

660 g (1 lb 7 oz/3 cups) sugar

a pinch of cream of tartar

½ teaspoon rosewater

1½ teaspoons liquid orange food colouring

Put the flour and rice flour into a large bowl. Put the yeast and 125 ml (4 fl oz/½ cup) lukewarm water into a small bowl and leave for a few minutes to soften, then stir to dissolve. Leave in a warm place for 10 minutes, or until the mixture starts to froth. This is to test whether the yeast is live; if it does not froth, start again with a fresh batch of yeast.

Gently heat the saffron strands in a frying pan over low heat for 1–2 minutes, shaking the pan frequently and taking care they don't burn. Remove to a plate to cool and crisp, then crush to a powder in a cup, adding the boiling water to dissolve. Pour the dissolved yeast and saffron water into a measuring pitcher. Add enough water to make up 625 ml (21 fl oz/2½ cups).

Stirring with a wooden spoon, add the measured liquid to the flour and beat well until the batter is very smooth. Add the yoghurt and beat again. Leave to rest for 1 hour, or until the batter starts to become frothy. You will need to beat vigorously again before starting to cook.

To make the syrup, put the sugar, cream of tartar and 750 ml (25½ fl oz/3 cups) water into a saucepan over low heat, stirring until the sugar has dissolved. Bring to the boil and boil for 8 minutes, or until the syrup is just thick enough to spin a thread. Remove from the heat, allow to cool until lukewarm, then flavour with rosewater and add the orange food colouring to brighten.

Heat the oil in a large heavy-based saucepan over medium heat. When the oil is hot, use a funnel to pour in the batter, making circles or figures of eight, and deep-fry, turning once, until crisp and golden on both sides. Lift out using a slotted spoon, and drain on paper towel, then lower the hot jalebis into the syrup and soak it for a minute or two. Lift out of the syrup (using another slotted spoon) and put on a plate to drain. Repeat until all the mixture is used. Transfer the jalebis to a clean plate and serve as soon as possible after making (though they should not be served hot) because their crispness diminishes after some time.

Gajjar Halwa
Carrot sweetmeat

Makes: about 20 pieces

60 g (2 oz) ghee
500 g (1 lb 2 oz) carrots, peeled and grated
¼ teaspoon ground cardamom
275 g (9½ oz/2¼ cups) sugar
250 g (8½ fl oz/1 cup) pouring (single/light) cream
4 tablespoons dried milk powder or khoa (page 15)
2 tablespoons slivered blanched almonds or pistachio nuts
edible silver leaf to garnish (optional)

Heat the ghee in a heavy-based saucepan over medium heat. Add the carrot and cardamom and cook, stirring to coat in the ghee, then reduce the heat to low, cover, and cook until the carrots are soft and almost all the liquid has been absorbed.

Meanwhile, put the sugar and 125 ml (4 fl oz/½ cup) hot water in a saucepan over low heat and stir until the sugar has dissolved.

Add the sugar syrup to the carrot mixture, then add the cream and milk powder, continue cooking and stir vigorously until the mixture is dry and comes away from the side of the pan. Remove from the heat and pour into a lightly buttered serving dish; allow to cool. Decorate the top with the slivered almonds and silver leaf, if using. Cut into diamond shapes or squares to serve.

Nan Khatai
Crisp semolina shortbread

Makes: about 24

These little shortbread biscuits (cookies) made with ghee have a delightful melting texture.

125 g (4½ oz) ghee

110 g (4 oz/½ cup) sugar

125 g (4½ oz/1 cup) fine semolina, sifted

35 g (1¼ oz/¼ cup) plain (all-purpose) flour, sifted

1 teaspoon ground cardamom

Preheat the oven to 150°C (300°F). Lightly grease 2 baking trays.

Cream the ghee and sugar together until light and pale. Add the semolina, flour and cardamom and mix well. Allow the mixture to stand for 30 minutes.

Take a scant tablespoon of the mixture at a time and roll into a ball. Place onto the prepared trays and flatten slightly. Repeat to make about 24 biscuits (cookies), leaving a little space between each so they can spread. Bake for 30 minutes, or until pale golden. Remove from the oven and allow to cool on the trays for 10 minutes, before transferring to a wire rack to cool completely. Store in an airtight container for up to 2 weeks.

Shahi Tukri
Toast of the shah

Serves: 6

80–120 g (2¾–4½ oz) ghee

6 thick slices of white bread, crusts removed

¼ teaspoon saffron strands

375 ml (12½ fl oz/1½ cups) milk

250 ml (8½ fl oz/1 cup) pouring (single/
light) cream

220 g (8 oz/1 cup) sugar

¼ teaspoon ground cardamom

1 tablespoon rosewater

1 tablespoon slivered blanched almonds

1 tablespoon slivered blanched
pistachio nuts

Heat the ghee in a large heavy-based frying pan over low heat and fry the bread until golden on both sides – it may be necessary to add more ghee. Remove to a plate.

Gently heat the saffron strands in a dry frying pan over low heat for a minute or two, shaking the pan frequently and taking care they don't burn. Remove to a plate to cool and crisp, then crush to a powder in a cup. Heat 1 tablespoon of the milk and stir to dissolve.

Put the milk and cream in the pan in which the bread was fried. Bring to the boil, then add the sugar and saffron mixture and boil vigorously, stirring constantly, for 10 minutes. Add the fried bread slices in one layer and simmer over low heat until the milk has been absorbed, carefully turning the slices of bread once during cooking.

Transfer the bread to a heated serving dish, sprinkle with the cardamom and rosewater and decorate with the slivered nuts. Serve hot.

Seviyan
Sweet vermicelli

Serves: 4–6

This traditional Muslim dish is served during the Eid Festival and would, on occasions like this, be garnished with edible silver leaf and pistachio nuts. Look in Indian grocery stores for the golden roasted wheat vermicelli with its extremely fine, hair-like strands.

125 g (4½ oz) fine roasted vermicelli

1½ tablespoons ghee

¼ teaspoon saffron strands

110 g (4 oz/½ cup) sugar

2 tablespoons sultanas (golden raisins) (optional)

2 tablespoons slivered almonds

⅛ teaspoon ground cardamom

300 ml (10 fl oz) pouring (single/light) cream

Break the vermicelli into small pieces less than 2.5 cm (1 in) in length. They need not be uniform, but longer pieces make stirring difficult.

Heat the ghee in a heavy-based saucepan over medium heat. Add the vermicelli and cook until golden brown, stirring so it colours evenly. Add 310 ml (10½ fl oz/1¼ cups) hot water and the saffron and bring to the boil, then reduce the heat to low, cover, and simmer until the vermicelli is cooked. Add the sugar and sultanas and continue simmering until all the liquid is absorbed. Stir in the almonds and cardamom and serve warm with the cream.

Boondi

Serves: 20

This popular sweet consists of hundreds of tiny balls of batter fried until crisp, then soaked in a saffron-flavoured syrup scented with cardamom and enriched with pistachio nuts. The syrup dries and crystallises around the fragments of batter so it may be eaten like sugar-coated peanuts, but with an infinitely more exotic flavour. It is for between-meal nibbling or a tea-time treat, and is not a dessert.

110 g (4 oz/1 cup) besan (chickpea flour) or combined half plain (all-purpose) flour and half rice flour, sifted

80 ml (2½ fl oz/⅓ cup) milk

½ teaspoon saffron strands

1 tablespoon boiling water

330 g (11½ oz/1½ cups) sugar

¼ teaspoon ground cardamom

oil for deep-frying

60 g (2 oz) ghee

1 tablespoon blanched pistachio nuts, thinly sliced

To make the batter, put the besan into a bowl. Put the milk and 60 ml (2 fl oz/¼ cup) water in a saucepan and heat until just lukewarm.

Gently heat the saffron strands in a dry frying pan over low heat for a minute or two, shaking the pan frequently and taking care they don't burn. Remove to a plate to cool and crisp, then crush to a powder in a cup, adding the boiling water and stirring to dissolve.

Add half of the saffron water to the milk and water in the pan and stir well, then add to the flour and beat well with a wooden spoon to form a thick smooth batter. Allow to stand for about 15 minutes.

Meanwhile, put the sugar and 375 ml (12½ fl oz/1½ cups) water into a wide saucepan and bring to the boil. Boil steadily until it reaches one-thread consistency (104°C/ 219°F on a candy thermometer). This should take about 8 minutes of vigorous boiling. Remove from the heat, add the remaining saffron water and the ground cardamom and stir to combine. Keep warm until ready to serve.

Heat the oil and ghee in a large heavy-based saucepan over medium heat. Take a slotted spoon or ladle with small round perforations and place it over the frying pan, then pour a spoonful of the batter into it and tap or shake so that the batter falls in small drops into the hot oil. Deep-fry for a few minutes until golden, then drain on another frying spoon and transfer them to the syrup. Continue frying the batter in batches and adding the boondi to the syrup. When all the batter has been fried, drained and added to the syrup, stir in the pistachios and mix together.

Allow to cool completely, stirring occasionally to separate the balls of batter. Another way of serving these is to make laddu boondi. In this case the mixture is not allowed to get quite cold, but is pressed to form large balls while still warm and sticky, then left to dry and harden before serving.

Ras Gula
Cream cheese balls in syrup

Serves: 6

One of the most popular Indian sweetmeats, ras gula means, literally, balls of juice. Small balls of homemade cream cheese are simmered in sugar syrup infused with intriguing flavours.

1.5 litres (51 fl oz/6 cups) milk

3–4 tablespoons lemon juice

1 tablespoon fine semolina

10–12 sugar cubes

440 g (15½ oz/2 cups) sugar

10–12 shelled pistachio nuts

10–12 cardamom seeds

8 cardamom pods, bruised

2 tablespoons rosewater

Put the milk into a large saucepan and bring almost to boiling point. As the milk starts to rise in the pan, remove from the heat and stir in the lemon juice. Allow to stand for 5 minutes, or until solid lumps form. If the milk does not curdle (lemons vary in acid content), re-heat the milk and add more lemon juice. Pour into a large colander lined with a large square of muslin (cheesecloth) and weigh down with a plate to press out as much liquid as possible. Drain for 30 minutes, or until the whey has dripped out.

Turn the curds out onto a clean work surface and knead for 5 minutes, using the heel of your hand. Add the semolina and knead again until the cream cheese is smooth. When the palm of your hand becomes greasy the cheese is ready for moulding. Shape into 10–12 balls with a 5 cm (2 in) diameter, moulding each one around a cube of sugar, a pistachio nut and a single cardamom seed.

Put the sugar and 1 litre (34 fl oz/4 cups) water in a large saucepan over low heat and stir until the sugar has dissolved. Bring to the boil and boil for 5 minutes. Put the ras gulas and bruised cardamom pods into the syrup in the saucepan and bring to the boil. Reduce the heat to low and simmer for about 1 hour, or until the balls swell and become spongy. Remove from the heat and allow to cool until lukewarm, then add the rosewater. Serve one or two ras gulas to each person, warm or at room temperature.

Ras Malai
Fresh cream cheese balls in cream

Serves: 6

Ras malai is regarded as the richest and most delicious of Indian desserts. It is actually a combination of two other sweet dishes, ras gula and rabri.

1 quantity Ras gula (page 186)

2 litres (68 fl oz/8 cups) milk

110 g (4 oz/½ cup) caster (superfine) sugar

a few drops kewra essence (glossary) or
   1 tablespoon rosewater

½ teaspoon natural almond extract

2 tablespoons pistachio nuts

To make ras malai, proceed with ras gula recipe on page 186, but instead of making 10 walnut-sized balls, divide the mixture into 18 even-sized balls and mould them without the sugar inside.

Simmer in the syrup as before, keeping the syrup from becoming too thick. When they are cooked and spongy, drain them from the syrup and immerse them in the milk. Leave to become quite cool. Remove the balls of cream cheese from the milk and set aside.

Now use this milk to make Rabri (page 172), but instead of reducing it to a third of its original volume, reduce it to only half so that it is thinner and not so concentrated. Remove from the heat. Add the caster sugar, kewra essence and almond extract. Stir to dissolve the sugar. Return the cream cheese balls to this mixture, cover and refrigerate. Sprinkle over the pistachio nuts and serve chilled.

Gulab Jamun
Rose-flavoured sweetmeats in syrup

Makes: about 20

135 g (5 oz/1⅓ cups) full-cream milk powder

60 g (2 oz) self-raising flour

¼ teaspoon bicarbonate of soda (baking soda)

¼ teaspoon ground cardamom

20 g (¾ oz) soft butter or ghee

ghee or oil for deep-frying

Syrup

440 g (15½ oz/2 cups) sugar

5 cardamom pods, bruised

2 tablespoons rosewater

Sift the milk powder, flour, bicarbonate of soda and cardamom into a large bowl. Rub in the butter, then add just enough water to make a firm but pliable dough which can be moulded into balls the size of large marbles, or into small sausage shapes.

To make the syrup, put the sugar, 1 litre (34 fl oz/4 cups) water and the cardamom pods in a saucepan over low heat and stir until the sugar has dissolved. Remove from the heat.

Heat the ghee in a large heavy-based saucepan over medium heat. When the oil is hot, deep-fry the balls until they turn light golden. Drain on paper towel.

Put the fried gulab jamun into the syrup and soak until they have almost doubled in size, and are soft and spongy. Add the rosewater when they have cooled slightly. Allow to cool completely and serve at room temperature or refrigerate briefly and serve slightly chilled.

Koulfi
Frozen dessert

Serves: 8

There is no ice cream quite like koulfi, with its cold smoothness punctuated by little lumps of cream and pieces of pistachio nut and almond. If one memory persists, it is of the itinerant vendor with the tin cones packed in crushed ice, shaking out a serving of the delicious rich, very cold ice cream, watching it slide from the mould onto the plate I held. It is not just a childhood memory – koulfi is colder than commercial ice cream, having no gelatine content and not being beaten and aerated, it freezes quite solid and must be eaten before it melts. The pieces of thick cream are a delight to come upon, and even if it is not made in the traditional tin cones, koulfi out of a freezer tray is well worth experiencing.

2 litres (68 fl oz/8 cups) milk

2 tablespoons arrowroot or cornflour (cornstarch)

165 g (6 oz/¾ cup) sugar

250 ml (8½ fl oz/1 cup) thick (double/ heavy) cream

a few drops of kewra essence or rosewater, to flavour

2 tablespoons blanched almonds, finely chopped

2 tablespoons blanched pistachio nuts, finely chopped

In a bowl, mix a little of the milk with the arrowroot to make a smooth paste.

Put 1.5 litres (51 fl oz/6 cups) of the milk into a saucepan and bring to the boil, stirring with a wooden spoon for 10 minutes. Remove from the heat and stir in the arrowroot paste until well combined. Place over low heat and stir constantly while returning to the boil. When it boils and thickens, add the sugar and stir until it has completely dissolved. Remove from the heat and allow to cool, stirring occasionally to prevent a skin forming on top.

Meanwhile, put the remaining milk into a large heavy-based frying pan and bring to the boil, stirring constantly, until the milk resembles a thick batter. Remove from the heat and allow to cool.

Once cool, stir this into the milk mixture. Add the cream. (The best kind of cream to use is that skimmed from the top of the milk during boiling. In some Middle Eastern shops this is sold as *ashtar*.)

Flavour the custard with the kewra essence, a drop or two at a time, taking care not to add too much. Stir in the almonds and pistachio nuts, then pour into freezer trays and freeze until firm, stirring once or twice during the freezing process to keep the nuts and cream spread evenly through the mixture.

Just before serving, cut into small 6 cm (2½ in) squares and top with a spoonful each of Rose syrup (page 195) and Agar-agar jelly (page 196) cut into small dice.

Firni
Rice blancmange

Serves: 4

750 ml (25½ fl oz/3 cups) milk

1 tablespoon rice flour

1 tablespoon sugar

½ teaspoon ground cardamom

1 tablespoon rosewater

2 tablespoons blanched pistachio nuts or almonds, chopped

In a bowl mix some of the milk with the rice flour to make a smooth paste.

Put the remaining milk and the sugar in a saucepan and bring to the boil, stirring with a wooden spoon. Remove from the heat and stir in the rice flour paste, then return the pan to the heat and stir constantly until the mixture boils and thickens. Boil, stirring, for 3 minutes. Remove from the heat. Sprinkle over the cardamom, rosewater and half of the pistachio nuts and stir well to combine.

Remove from the heat and pour the mixture into individual serving dishes. Decorate with the remaining pistachio nuts. Serve warm or chilled.

Drinks

✤

Zeera Pani
Cumin and tamarind water

Makes: 500 ml (17 fl oz/2 cups)

Cumin is reputed to be a digestive, and this refreshing sour drink is served as an appetiser, much as tomato juice is in other countries. It is also served with festive, and therefore very rich, meals. Serve it chilled with crushed ice, a sprig of mint and a slice of lemon to garnish.

125 g (4½ oz/½ cup) tamarind pulp

3 teaspoons finely grated fresh ginger

2 teaspoons ground cumin

a pinch of chilli powder (optional)

½ teaspoon garam masala (page 19)

3 teaspoons sugar, or to taste

salt to taste

iced water and crushed ice to serve

mint sprigs to serve

lemon slices to garnish

Soak the tamarind pulp in 500 ml (17 fl oz/2 cups) hot water and leave for 10 minutes. Squeeze to dissolve the pulp in the water, then strain, discarding the seeds and fibres.

Add all the remaining ingredients, stir well, then strain again through a very fine sieve. Refrigerate until cold, then dilute with iced water at serving time. Serve in glasses with the crushed ice, mint and lemon slices.

Note

If you cannot get the dried tamarind pulp, use tamarind purée but increase the quantity according to taste. It should be quite tangy.

Sharbat Gulab
Rose-flavoured cold drink

Makes: 750 ml (25½ fl oz/3 cups) cold syrup

Rose syrup

660 g (1 lb 7 oz/3 cups) sugar

60 ml (2 fl oz/¼ cup) rosewater

1 teaspoon liquid red food colouring

1 teaspoon tulsi seeds (glossary)

iced water and crushed ice to serve

To make the rose syrup, put the sugar and 500 ml (17 fl oz/2 cups) water into a saucepan and cook over gentle heat until the sugar has dissolved. Cool. Add the rosewater and red food colouring – it should have a strong colour, as it will be mixed with a large proportion of water.

Soak the tulsi seeds in a cup of cold water. After a few minutes they will develop a jelly-like coating. (The seeds can be kept soaking in the refrigerator for up to 1 week. They are supposed to have a very cooling effect, and are used in almost every type of sharbat drink.)

At serving time put 2 tablespoons of syrup in each glass and fill up with iced water and crushed ice. The syrup can be increased or decreased according to taste. Add a spoonful of soaked tulsi seeds.

Falooda

Makes: as many as required

There are many versions of falooda – this one is a favourite. It is a sweet drink ideal for serving with curry meals. It gets its name from the particles of cornflour (cornstarch) vermicelli that float in it, but these, which are difficult to make without specialist equipment, are often replaced with tiny pieces of jelly or cooked tapioca. Another easy substitute is cellophane (bean thread) noodles soaked and boiled until soft and translucent, then cut into short lengths. Falooda can be served as a dessert or as a refreshing drink. In this version a rose-flavoured syrup is mixed with ice-cold milk, crushed ice and jewel-like squares of sparkling red and green agar-agar jelly in tall glasses.

Agar-agar used to be available in powder form by the gram or ounce from chemists, but you will be surer to find it in packets in Asian grocery stores. It is popular in Asia for making jellies and sweetmeats because it sets without refrigeration.

1 quantity Rose syrup (page 195)

ice-cold milk, about 250 ml (8½ fl oz/1 cup) per serving

crushed iced to serve

soaked tulsi seeds (optional)

Agar-agar jelly

1 tablespoon agar-agar powder or 1 cup agar-agar strands soaked for 2 hours in cold water, then drained

125 g (4½ oz) sugar

2 tablespoons rosewater, or to taste

1 teaspoon liquid red food colouring

1 teaspoon liquid green food colouring

To make the jelly, put 750 ml (25½ fl oz/3 cups) water into a saucepan and sprinkle over the agar-agar powder. Bring to the boil, then reduce the heat and simmer for 10 minutes, or until the agar-agar has dissolved. Add the sugar and stir to dissolve, then remove from the heat, cool slightly and add the rosewater. Divide the mixture between two large shallow dishes and colour one red and the other green. Leave to set. When quite cold and firm, cut into small dice.

Put 2 tablespoons each of red and green jelly into each tall glass with the rose syrup. Fill with milk and crushed ice. If liked, some soaked tulsi seeds can be floated on top.

Lassi
Yoghurt drink

Makes: 750 ml (25½ fl oz/3 cups)

You can also make this refreshing drink with buttermilk. Use twice as much as yoghurt and add less water.

125 g (4½ oz/½ cup) plain yoghurt

375 ml (12½ fl oz/1½ cups) iced water

pepper and salt to taste

ice cubes to serve

Put the yoghurt into a deep pitcher and beat with a spoon to take any lumps out of it. Add the water, gradually at first, mixing well. Season to taste with salt and pepper and serve in glasses with ice cubes.

Variation

You can make a sweet version of this lassi by stirring 1–2 tablespoons sugar into the yoghurt before adding the iced water. Afterwards, if desired, flavour with 1 teaspoon rosewater or a pinch of ground cardamom before serving.

Mango Lassi

Makes: 500 ml (17 fl oz/2 cups)

This mango lassi is a popular drink, especially with children. It will froth and look like a milkshake, and is generally acceptable even to those who do not like yoghurt by itself. You may prefer to use lemonade instead of soda water (club soda) – in which case, omit the sugar.

95 g (3¼ oz/½ cup) finely chopped mango

2 tablespoons plain yoghurt

2 teaspoons sugar

375 ml (12½ fl oz/1½ cups) iced soda water (club soda)

Put the mango in a blender with the yoghurt, sugar and 125 ml (4 fl oz/½ cup) of the soda water and mix well to combine. Add the remainder of the soda water and use a spoon to stir through. Serve in glasses with ice cubes.

Glossary

and

Index

*

Agar-agar

A setting agent obtained from seaweed, agar-agar is widely used in Asia, as it sets without refrigeration. It is sold in sachets in powder form and is available from Asian grocery stores and health food stores. It is also sold in strands, though they are less obtainable and slower to dissolve. Also known as: *kyauk kyaw* (Burma), *dai choy goh* (China), *kanten* (Japan), *gulaman* (Philippines), *chun chow* (Sri Lanka), *woon* (Thailand), *rau cau* (Vietnam).

Ajowan
Botanical name: *Carum ajowan*

Of the same family as parsley and cumin, ajowan or ajwain seeds look like parsley or celery seeds, but have the flavour of thyme. Ajowan is used in Indian cooking, particularly in lentil dishes that provide the protein in vegetarian diets, both as a flavouring and as a carminative (relieves flatulence). It is one of the ingredients used to flavour crisp-fried snacks made from lentil flour. Ajowan water is used as a remedy for stomach ailments.

Amchur powder

Dried green (unripe) mango. Available in powder form, amchur is used as an acidic flavouring ingredient in Indian cooking. Other spellings: *amchoor*.

Asafoetida
Botanical name: *Ferula asafoetida*

Used in minute quantities in Indian cooking. It is obtained from the resinous gum of a plant that grows in Afghanistan and Iran. The stalks are cut close to the root and the milky fluid that flows out is dried into the resin sold as asafoetida. Although it has quite an unpleasant smell by itself, traditionally a tiny piece the size of a pea is attached to the inside of the lid of a cooking pot – this adds depth of flavour and is said to prevent flatulence. If you cannot get the actual resin, use the powdered form, which has been mixed with ground rice, and add with other spices. Also known as: sheingho (Burma), hing or perunkaya (India).

Atta flour

Fine wholemeal (whole-wheat) flour used in making Indian flatbreads. Substitute fine wholemeal flour sold in health food stores or Asian grocery stores.

Besan (chickpea flour)

Available at most large supermarkets and Asian grocery stores. Pea flour from health food stores can be substituted, but if it is coarse, pass it through a fine sieve before using. Alternatively, roast yellow split peas in a heavy-based frying pan, stirring constantly and taking care not to burn them. Cool, then process in a food processor or pound using a mortar and pestle, sift, then store the fine flour in an airtight container. Besan has a distinctive taste, and ordinary wheat flour cannot be substituted.

Bombay duck

Not a bird, despite its name, this is a variety of fish that is salted and dried. It is sold in packets and should be cut into pieces no more than 2.5 cm (1 in) long before using. Deep-fried or grilled, it is served as an accompaniment to a meal of rice and curry, and should be nibbled in little pieces.

Cardamom
Botanical name: *Elettaria cardamomum*

Next to saffron, cardamom is the world's most expensive spice. Cardamoms grow mainly in India and Sri Lanka, and are the seed pods of a member of the ginger family. The dried seed pods are either pale green or brown, according to variety; sometimes they are bleached white. They are added, either whole or bruised, to pilaus and other rice dishes, spiced curries and other preparations or sweets. When ground cardamom is called for, the seed pods are opened and discarded and only the small black or brown seeds are ground. For full flavour, it is best to grind them just before using. If you cannot buy a high-quality ground cardamom, crush the seeds using a mortar and pestle or spice mill, as required. Also known as: *phalazee* (Burma), *illaichi* (India), *kapulaga* (Indonesia), *buah pelaga* (Malaysia), *enasal* (Sri Lanka), *kravan* (Thailand).

Chillies, green and red
Botanical name: *Capsicum* spp.

Chillies mature from green to red, becoming hotter as they mature. Both varieties are used fresh for flavouring, either whole or finely chopped, sliced as a garnish or ground into sambals. The seeds, which are the hottest parts, are usually (though not always) removed. Larger varieties tend to be milder than the small varieties. See page 8 for handling. Dried red chillies are found in packets in Asian grocery stores – the medium- to large-sized chillies are best for most recipes in this book.

Chilli powder

Asian chilli powder is made from ground chillies. It is much hotter than the Mexican-style chilli powder, which is mostly ground cumin. You may be able to find ground Kashmiri chillies, which are a brighter red colour and not as hot as other ground chillies.

Cinnamon
Botanical name: *Cinnamomum zeylanicum* and *verum*

True cinnamon is native to Sri Lanka. Buy cinnamon sticks or quills rather than the ground spice, which loses its flavour when stored too long. It is used in both sweet and savoury dishes. Cassia, which is grown in India, Indonesia and Burma, is similar. It is much stronger in flavour, and is cheaper, but it lacks the delicacy of cinnamon. The leaves and buds of the cassia tree have a flavour similar to the bark and are also used for flavouring food. For sweet dishes, use true cinnamon. Cassia bark is much thicker because the corky layer is left on. Also known as: *thit-ja-boh-guak* (Burma), *darchini* (India), *kayu manis* (Malaysia and Indonesia), *kurundu* (Sri Lanka), *op chery* (Thailand), *que* (Vietnam).

Cloves
Botanical name: *Syzygium aromaticum, Eugenia aromatica* and *E. caryophyllus*

Cloves are the dried flower buds of an evergreen tropical tree native to Southeast Asia. They were used in China more than 2000 years ago, and were also used by the Romans. Oil of cloves contains phenol, a powerful antiseptic that discourages putrefaction, and the clove is hence one of the spices that helps preserve food. Also known as: *ley-nyin-bwint* (Burma), *laung* (India), *cengkeh* (Indonesia), *bunga cingkeh* (Malaysia), *karabu* (Sri Lanka), *kaan ploo* (Thailand).

Glossary ❖

Coconut milk

This is not the water inside the nut, as is commonly believed, but the creamy liquid extracted from the grated flesh of fresh coconuts or from desiccated or shredded coconut (pages 6–8). When coconut milk is called for, especially in sweet dishes, do make an effort to use it, for its flavour cannot be duplicated by using any other kind of milk. Tinned and Tetra Pak coconut milk saves time and effort, although be warned that some brands are far better than others so try a few until you find one that appeals. Low-fat coconut milk is an unappealing substitute.

Coriander (cilantro)

Botanical name: *Coriandrum sativum*

All parts of the coriander plant are used in Asian cooking. The dried seed is the main ingredient in curry powder and, although not hot, it has a fragrance that makes it an essential part of a curry blend. The fresh coriander herb is also known as cilantro or Chinese parsley in other parts of the world. It is indispensable in Burma, Thailand, Vietnam, Cambodia, India and China where it is also called 'fragrant green'. Also known as: *nannamzee* (seed), *nannambin* (leaves) (Burma), *chee van soy* (Cambodia), *yuen sai* (China), *dhania* (seed), *dhania pattar, dhania sabz* (leaves) (India), *phak hom pom* (Laos), *ketumbar* (seeds), *daun ketumbar* (leaves) (Malaysia), *kinchay* (Philippines), *kottamalli* (seed), *kottamalli kolle* (leaves) (Sri Lanka), *pak chee* (Thailand), *ngò, rau mùi* (Vietnam).

Cumin

Botanical name: *Cuminum cyminum*

Cumin is, with coriander, the most essential ingredient in prepared curry powders. It is available as seed, or ground. There may be some confusion between cumin and caraway seeds because they are similar in appearance, but the flavours are completely different and one cannot replace the other in recipes. Also known as: *ma-ch'in* (China), *sufaid zeera* (white cumin), *zeera, jeera* (India), *jinten* (Indonesia), *kumin* (Japan), *jintan puteh* (Malaysia), *sududuru* (Sri Lanka), *yira* (Thailand).

Cumin, black

See nigella.

Curry leaves

Botanical name: *Murraya koenigii*

Sold fresh or dried, they are as important to curries as bay leaves are to stews, but never try to substitute one for the other. The tree is native to Asia, the leaves are small, pointed and shiny, growing in opposing pairs along a central stalk. Although they keep their flavour well when dried or frozen, they are found in such abundance in Asia that they are generally used fresh. The tree is easy to grow from seed even in a temperate climate. The leaves are fried in oil until crisp at the start of preparing a curry. Dried curry leaves can be pulverised using a mortar and pestle; and the powdered leaves can be used in marinades and omelettes. Also known as: *pyi-naw-thein* (Burma), *kitha neem, katnim, karipattar, karuvepila* (India), *daun kari, karupillay* (Malaysia), *karapincha* (Sri Lanka).

Curry powder

Rarely used in countries where curry is eaten daily (the word comes from the Tamil *kari*, meaning 'sauce'). It is preferable to roast and grind the spices separately. (See notes on Indian curry powders and pastes, page 16.)

Fennel

Botanical name: *Foeniculum vulgare*

Sometimes known as 'sweet cumin' or 'large cumin', because of its similar-shaped seeds, it is a member of the same botanical family and is used in Sri Lankan curries (but in much smaller quantities than true cumin). It is available in ground or seed form. Substitute an equal amount of aniseed. Also known as: *samouk-saba* (Burma), *sonf* (India), *adas* (Indonesia), *jintan manis* (Malaysia), *maduru* (Sri Lanka), *yira* (Thailand).

Fenugreek

Botanical name: *Trigonella foenum-graecum*

These small, flat, squarish, brownish-beige seeds are essential in curries, but because they have a slightly bitter flavour they must be used in the stated quantities. They are especially good in fish and seafood curries, where the whole seeds are gently fried at the start of cooking; they are also ground and added to curry powders. The green leaves are used in Indian cooking and, when spiced, the bitter taste is quite piquant and acceptable. The plant is easy to grow and, when at the two-leaf stage, the sprouts make a tangy addition to salads. Also known as: *methi* (India), *alba* (Malaysia), *uluhaal* (Sri Lanka).

Galangal, lesser (aromatic ginger)

Botanical name: *Kaempferia pandurata, Alpinia officinarum*

Also known as 'aromatic ginger', this member of the ginger family cannot be used as a substitute for ginger or vice versa. It is used only in certain dishes and gives a pronounced aromatic flavour. When available fresh, it is sliced or pounded to a pulp; but outside of Asia it is usually sold dried, and the hard round slices must be pounded using a mortar and pestle or pulverised in a food processor before use. In some spice ranges it is sold in powdered form as kencur powder. The plant is native to southern China and has been used for centuries in medicinal herbal mixtures, but it is not used in Chinese cooking. Also known as: *sa leung geung, sha geung fun* (China), *kencur* (Indonesia), *zeodary* or *kencur* (Malaysia), *ingurupiyali* (Sri Lanka), *krachai* (Thailand).

Garam masala

Garam masala is one of the best known Indian spice blends. There are many versions, but see page 19 for the recipes that I use.

Ghee (Clarified Butter)

Sold in tins, ghee is pure butterfat without any of the milk solids. It can be heated to much higher temperatures than butter without burning, and imparts a distinctive flavour when used as a cooking medium. See page 15 for details on making ghee.

Ginger

Botanical name: *Zingiber officinale*

A rhizome with a robust flavour and a warming quality, it is essential in most Asian dishes. Fresh ginger root should be used; powdered ginger cannot be substituted for fresh ginger, because the flavour is quite different. To prepare for use, scrape off the skin with a sharp knife and either grate or chop finely (according to recipe requirements) before measuring. To preserve fresh ginger for long periods of time, place in a freezer bag and store in the freezer – it is a simple matter to peel and grate in the frozen state. Also known as: *gin* (Burma), *khnyahee* (Cambodia), *jeung* (China), *adrak* (India), *jahe* (Indonesia), *shoga* (Japan), *halia* (Malaysia), *luya* (Philippines), *inguru* (Sri Lanka), *khing* (Thailand), *gung* (Vietnam).

Kencur (aromatic ginger) powder
See Galangal, lesser (aromatic ginger).

Kewra essence
Used mostly in Indian sweets, it comes from a variety of pandanus (*Pandanus odoratissimus*). The male inflorescence has a stronger perfume than roses or jasmine. Kewra essence is so strong that only a drop is needed (or, more discreetly, a small skewer dipped in the essence is swished in the liquid to be flavoured). On special festive occasions, rose essence and kewra essence are used to flavour the rich rice dish, biriani.

Khoa
Khoa is unsweetened condensed milk, usually made at home by cooking milk until the water content is almost totally evaporated. It is often used in Indian sweets.

Mace
Botanical name: *Myristica fragrans*

Mace is part of the nutmeg, a fruit that looks like an apricot and grows on tall tropical trees. When ripe, the fruit splits to reveal the aril, lacy and bright scarlet, surrounding the shell of the seed; the dried aril is mace and the kernel is nutmeg. Mace has a flavour similar to nutmeg but more delicate, and it is sometimes used in meat or fish curries, especially in Sri Lanka, although its main use in Asia is medicinal (a few blades of mace steeped in hot water, the water then being taken to combat nausea and diarrhoea). Also known as: *javatri* (India), *wasa-vasi* (Sri Lanka).

Malai
Malai is clotted cream, not separated cream, and collected from the top of boiled and cooled milk. Milk is boiled in a pan and then cooled. The skin is collected from the top and the process is repeated.

Mint
Botanical name: *Mentha piperita*

Although there are many varieties, the common, round-leafed mint is the one most often used in cooking. It adds flavour to many dishes, and fresh mint chutney is an essential accompaniment to an Indian biriani meal or as a dipping sauce for samoosa. Mint is also used in Laotian fish dishes as well as Thai, Cambodian and Vietnamese salads. Also known as: *chee ongkaam* (Cambodia), *podina* (India), *pak hom ho* (Laos), *daun pudina* (Malaysia), *meenchi (Sri Lanka), hung cay* (Vietnam).

Mustard seeds, black
Botanical name: *Brassica nigra*

This variety of mustard seed is smaller and more pungent than the yellow variety. Substitute brown mustard seeds (*B. juncia*). Alba or white mustard seeds are not used in Asian cooking. Also known as: *rai, kimcea* (brown mustard) (India), *biji sawi* (Malaysia), *abba* (Sri Lanka).

Nigella
Botanical name: *Nigella sativa*

Although the Indian name *kala zeera* translates as 'black cumin', this is not true cumin and the flavour is different. The small, matt black seeds are similar in size and shape to sesame seeds, only slightly more angular. Aromatic and peppery, nigella is often used as a garnish on Indian breads and is an essential ingredient in *panch phora*. Also known as: *kala zeera, kalonji* (India).

Nutmeg
Botanical name: *Myristica fragrans*

Not widely used as a curry spice, but used to flavour some sweets and cakes, and sometimes used in garam masala. For maximum flavour, always grate finely just before using. Use sparingly, as large quantities (more than one whole nut) can be poisonous. Also known as: *zalipho thi* (Burma), *tau kau* (China), *jaiphal* (India), *pala* (Indonesia), *buah pala* (Malaysia), *sadikka* (Sri Lanka).

Panch phora
Panch means 'five' in Hindi. Panch phora is a combination of five different aromatic seeds. These are used whole, and when added to the cooking oil impart a flavour typical of Indian food.

Panir
In India, cheese is not the aged and fermented product of Western culture – it is a fresh, usually homemade, product called panir. Depending on the use for which it is required, it may be pressed to extract more moisture, or used in a softer form. See the recipe on page 15.

Paprika
Botanical name: *Capsicum tetragonum*

Paprika peppers can be tinned or bottled as pimiento, but are more often used dried and powdered and known simply as paprika. Good paprika should have a mild, sweet flavour and brilliant red colour. Although it is essentially a European flavouring, particularly used in Hungary and Poland, it is useful in Asian cooking for imparting the necessary red colour to a curry when the chilli tolerance of the diners is not very high. In Asia, the colour would come from 20 to 30 chillies!

Pepper, black
Botanical name: *Piper nigrum*

Pepper, the berry of a tropical vine native to India, is green when immature, and red or yellow when ripe. Black pepper is obtained by boiling and then sun-drying the green, unripe drupes. It is only used in some curries, but is an important ingredient in garam masala. Vietnam is the main producer of pepper. Also known as: *nga-youk-kaun* (Burma), *hu-chiao* (China), *kali mirich* (India), *merica hitam* (Indonesia), *kosho* (Japan), *phik noi* (Laos), *lada hitam* (Malaysia), *paminta* (Philippines), *gammiris* (Sri Lanka), *prik thai* (Thailand).

Poppy seeds
Used in Indian curries mainly for thickening sauces since flour, cornflour (cornstarch) or other starches are never used for thickening. The seeds are ground to a powder for this use. Also known as: *khas-khas* (India).

Rice, ground
This can be bought at supermarkets and health food stores. It is slightly more granular than rice flour. It gives a crisper texture when used in batters.

Rosewater

A favourite flavouring in Indian and Persian sweets, rosewater is the diluted essence extracted from rose petals by steam distillation. It is essential in Gulab jamun (page 189) and Ras gula (page 186), and is also used in biriani. If you use rose essence or concentrate, be careful not to over-flavour and be sure to count the drops. However, with rosewater a 1 tablespoon-measure can safely be used. Buy rosewater from chemists or from shops specialising in Asian or Middle Eastern ingredients.

Roti flour

Creamy in colour and slightly granular in texture, this is ideal flour for all unleavened breads; unlike atta flour, it is not made from the whole grain but instead the polished or milled grain. Sold at some health food stores and Chinese grocery stores as well as Indian grocery stores.

Saffron

Botanical name: *Crocus sativus*

The world's most expensive spice, saffron is obtained by drying the stamens of the saffron or autumn crocus. The thread-like strands are dark orange in colour and have a strong perfume; it is also available in powder form. Do not confuse it with turmeric, which is sometimes sold as 'Indian saffron'. Beware also of cheap saffron, which in all probability will be safflower or 'bastard saffron' – it looks similar, and imparts colour, but has none of the saffron fragrance. Saffron is used more extensively in northern India than anywhere else in Asia. Also known as: *kesar* (China), *zaffran*, *kesari* (India), *koma-koma* (Malaysia), *kasubha* (Philippines).

Semolina

A wheat product sometimes known as 'farina', it comes in coarse, medium and fine grades. Recipes stipulate the correct grade to use, but a different grade can be substituted although there will be some change in texture. The bulk semolina sold in health food stores is medium grade; and the packaged semolina sold in Italian grocery stores and delicatessens is either medium or very fine. A little experimental shopping is recommended, for the grade of semolina is seldom labelled.

Sesame oil

Sesame oil, also known as gingelly oil and til oil, is a very ancient ingredient, used centuries ago only by the rich for food, ointment and medicine. It is still used in India in Ayurvedic medicine. In Burma and some parts of India, sesame oil has long been the universal cooking medium and is what gives the typical flavour to foods of those regions, although fairly tasteless in itself. It may be a clear or golden colour compared to the darker, more aromatic oriental sesame oil used in China, Japan and Korea. If gingelly oil or til oil is unavailable, use the cold-pressed sesame oil from health food shops mixed with 20 per cent oriental (toasted) sesame oil, or use one part oriental sesame oil to three parts other flavourless vegetable oil, such as corn oil. Also known as: *hnan zi* (Burma), *ma yau* (China), *gingelly*, *til ka tel* (India), *goma abura* (Japan), *chan keh room* (Korea), *minyak bijan* (Malaysia), *thala tel* (Sri Lanka), *dau me* (Vietnam).

Spring roll pastry

Thin, white sheets of pliable pastry sold in plastic packets and kept frozen. Thaw and peel off one at a time (unused wrappers can be re-frozen). These can be used to make samoosa and singara.

Tamarind

Botanical name: *Tamarindus indica*

The tamarind is a sour-tasting fruit of a large tropical tree. It is shaped like a large broad (fava) bean and has a brittle brown shell, inside which are shiny dark seeds covered with tangy brown flesh. Tamarind is dried into a pulp and sold in packets, as well as diluted with water and sold as a purée. These can vary in concentration. The pulp needs to be soaked first in hot water, then squeezed until it breaks up and dissolves. It needs to be strained before using. May be substituted with lemon juice. Also known as: *ma-gyi-thi* (Burma), *ampil tum* (ripe), *ampil kheei* (green) (Cambodia), *imli* (India), *mal kham* (Laos), *asam* (Malaysia and Indonesia), *sampalok* (Philippines), *siyambala* (Sri Lanka), *som ma kham* (Thailand), *me* (Vietnam).

Tulsi (Holy basil)

Botanical name: *Ocimum sanctum*

The tiny black seed of the plant known as holy basil, so named because it is planted around temples. The seeds look like miniature black sesame seeds when dry, but soaked in water they develop a slippery, translucent coating. They are floated on cool, sweet drinks, for they are said to cool the body (a highly regarded attribute in hot countries). Although without flavour, they add an intriguing texture. Also known as: *kus kus* (Sri Lanka), *luk manglak, krapow* (Thailand).

Turmeric

Botanical name: *Curcuma longa*

A rhizome of the ginger family, turmeric, with its orange-yellow colour, is a mainstay of commercial curry powders. Though often called Indian saffron, it should never be confused with true saffron and the two may not be used interchangeably. Also known as: *fa nwin, sa nwin* (Burma), *romiet* (Cambodia), *wong geung fun* (China), *haldi* (India), *kunyit* (Indonesia), *ukon* (Japan), *kunyit* (Malaysia), *dilau* (Philippines), *kaha* (Sri Lanka), *khamin* (Thailand), *cú nghê, ngh* (Vietnam).

Yoghurt

For recipes in this book, use unflavoured (plain) yoghurt (preferably one with a pronounced acid flavour) such as Greek-style yoghurt or sheep's or goat's milk yoghurt.

INDEX